AN APOLOGY FC

BY

MICHEL DE MONTAIGNE

(28 February 1533 – 13 September 1592)

Translated by

Charles Cotton

(28 April 1630 – 16 February 1687)

Includes MLA Style Citations for Scholarly Secondary Sources, Peer-Reviewed Journal Articles and Critical Essays

An Apology for Raymond Sebond

by

Michel De Montaigne

(28 February 1533 – 13 September 1592)

Translated by

Charles Cotton

(28 April 1630 – 16 February 1687)

Includes MLA Style Citations for Scholarly Secondary Sources, Peer-Reviewed Journal Articles and Critical Essays

A Squid Ink Classic

[Squid Ink Classics Edition]

May 2017

Boston, MA

Learning is, indeed, a very great and a very material accomplishment; and those who despise it sufficiently discover their own want of understanding; but learning yet I do not prize it at the excessive rate that some others do, as Herillus, the philosopher, for one, who therein places the sovereign good, and maintained "That it was only in her to render us wise and contented," which I do not believe; no more than I do what others have said, that learning is the mother of all virtue, and that all vice proceeds from ignorance, which, if it be true, required a very long interpretation. My house has long-been open to men of knowledge, and is very well known to them; for my father, who governed it fifty years and upwards, inflamed with the new ardour with which Francis the First embraced letters, and brought them into esteem, with great diligence and expense hunted after the acquaintance of learned men, receiving them into his house as persons sacred, and that had some particular inspiration of divine wisdom; collecting their sayings and sentences as so many oracles, and with so much the greater reverence and religion as he was the less able to judge of them; for he had no knowledge of letters any more than his predecessors. For my part I love them well, but I do not adore them. Amongst others, Peter Bunel, a man of great reputation for knowledge in his time, having, with some others of his sort, staid some days at Montaigne in my father's company, he presented him at his departure with a book, entitled Theologia naturalis; sive Liber Creaturarum, magistri Raimondi de Sebonde. And as the Italian and Spanish tongues were familiar to my father, and as this book was written in a sort of jargon of Spanish with Latin terminations, he hoped that, with a little help, he might be able to understand it, and therefore recommended it to him for a very useful book, and proper tor the time wherein he gave it to him; which was when the novel doctrines of Luther began to be in vogue, and in many places to stagger our ancient belief: wherein he was very well advised, wisely, in his own reason, foreseeing that the beginning of this distemper would easily run into an execrable atheism, for the vulgar, not having the faculty of judging of things, suffering themselves to be carried away by chance and appearance, after having once been inspired with the boldness to despise and control those opinions which they had before had in extreme reverence, such as those wherein their salvation is concerned, and that some of the articles of their religion are brought into doubt and dispute, they afterwards throw all other parts of their belief into the same uncertainty, they having with them no other authority or foundation than the others they had already discomposed; and shake off all the impressions they had received from the authority of the laws, or the reverence of the ancient customs, as a tyrannical yoke:

Nam cupide eonculcatur nimis ante metutum;

"For with most eagerness they spurn the law,

By which they were before most kept in awe;"

resolving to admit nothing for the future to which they had not first interposed their own decrees, and given their particular consent.

It happened that my father, a little before his death, having accidentally found this book under a heap of other neglected papers, commanded me to translate it for him into French. It is good too translate such authors as this, where there is little but the matter itself to express; but such wherein grace of language and elegance of style are aimed at, are dangerous to attempt, especially when a man is to turn them into a weaker idiom. It was a strange and a new undertaking for me; but having by chance at that time nothing else to do, and not being able to resist the command of the best father that ever was, I did it as well as I could; and he was so well pleased with it as to order it to be printed, which after his death was done.

I found the ideas of this author exceeding fine the contexture of his work well followed, and his design full of piety; and because many people take a delight to read it, and particularly the ladies, to whom we owe the most service, I have often thought to assist them to clear the book of two principal objections made to it. His design is bold and daring, for he undertakes, by human and natural reasons, to establish and make good, against the atheists, all the articles of the Christian religion: wherein, to speak the truth, he is so firm and so successful that I do not think it possible to do better upon that subject; nay, I believe he has been equalled by none. This work seeming to me to be too beautiful and too rich for an author whose name is so little known, and of whom all that we know is that he was a Spaniard, practising physic at Toulouse about two hundred years ago; I enquired of Adrian Turnebus, who knew all things, what he thought of that book; who made answer, "That he thought it was some abstract drawn from St. Thomas d'Aquin; for that, in truth, his mind, so full of infinite erudition and admirable subtlety, was alone capable of such thoughts." Be this as it may, whoever was the author and inventor (and 'tis not reasonable, without greater certainty, to deprive Sebond of that title), he was a man of great judgment and most admirable parts.

The first thing they reprehend in his work is "That Christians are to blame to repose their belief upon human reason, which is only conceived by faith and the particular inspiration of divine grace." In which objection there appears to be something of zeal to piety, and therefore we are to endeavour to satisfy those who put it forth with the greater mildness and respect. This were a task more proper for a man well read in divinity than for me, who know nothing of it; nevertheless, I conceive that in a thing so divine, so high, and so far transcending all human intelligence, as is that truth, with which it has pleased the bounty of God to enlighten us, it is very necessary that he should moreover lend us his assistance, as a very extraordinary favour and privilege, to conceive and imprint it in our understanding. And I do not believe that means purely human are in any sort capable of doing it: for, if they were, so many rare and excellent souls, and so abundantly furnished with natural force, in former ages, could not have failed, by their reason, to arrive at this knowledge. 'Tis faith alone that livelily mind certainly comprehends the deep mysteries of our religion; but, withal, I do not say that it is not a worthy and very laudable attempt to accommodate those natural and human utensils with which God has endowed us to the service of our faith: it is not to be doubted but that it is the most noble use we can put them to; and that there is not a design in a Christian man more noble than to make it the aim and end of all his studies to extend and amplify the truth of his belief. We do not satisfy ourselves with serving God with our souls and understandings only, we moreover owe and render him a corporal reverence, and apply our limbs and motions, and external things to do him honour; we must here do the same, and accompany our faith with all the reason we have, but always with this reservation, not to fancy that it is upon us that it depends, nor that our arguments and endeavours can arrive at so supernatural and divine a knowledge. If it enters not into us by an extraordinary infusion; if it enters not only by reason, but, moreover, by human ways, it is not in us in its true dignity and splendour: and yet, I am afraid, we only have it by this way.

If we hold upon God by the mediation of a lively faith; if we hold upon God by him, and not by us; if we had a divine basis and foundation, human occasions would not have the power to shake us as they do; our fortress would not surrender to so weak a battery; the love of novelty, the constraint of princes, the success of one party, and the rash and fortuitous change of our opinions, would not have the power to stagger and alter our belief: we should not then leave it to the mercy of every new argument, nor abandon it to all the rhetoric in the world; we should withstand the fury of these waves with an immovable and unyielding constancy:

   As a great rock repels the rolling tides,

   That foam and bark about her marble sides,

   From its strong bulk

If we were but touched with this ray of divinity, it would appear throughout; not only our words, but our works also, would carry its brightness and lustre; whatever proceeded from us would be seen illuminated with this noble light. We ought to be ashamed that, in all the human sects, there never was any of the faction, that did not, in some measure, conform his life and behaviour to it, whereas so divine and heavenly an institution does only distinguish Christians by the name! Will you see the proof of this? Compare our manners to those of a Mahometan or Pagan, you will still find that we fall very

short; there, where, out of regard to the reputation and advantage of our religion, we ought to shine in excellency at a vast distance beyond all others: and that it should be said of us, "Are they so just, so charitable, so good: Then they are Christians." All other signs are common to all religions; hope, trust, events, ceremonies, penance,

martyrs. The peculiar mark of our truth ought to be our virtue, as it is also the most heavenly and difficult, and the most worthy product of truth. For this our good St. Louis was in the right, who, when the Tartar king, who was become Christian, designed to come to Lyons to kiss the Pope's feet, and there to be an eye-witness of the sanctity he hoped to find in our manner, immediately diverted him from his purpose; for fear lest our disorderly way of living should, on the contrary, put him out of conceit with so holy a belief! And yet it happened quite otherwise since to that other, who, going to Rome, to the same end, and there seeing the dissoluteness of the prelates and people of that time, settled himself so much the more firmly in our religion, considering how great the force and divinity of it must necessarily be that could maintain its dignity and splendour among so much corruption, and in so vicious hands. If we had but one single grain of faith, we should remove mountains from their places, saith the sacred Word; our actions, that would then be directed and accompanied by the divinity, would not be merely human, they would have in them something of miraculous, as well as our belief: Brevis est institutio vit honest beauque, si credos. "Believe, and the way to happiness and virtue is a short one." Some impose upon the world that they believe that which they do not; others, more in number, make themselves believe that they believe, not being able to penetrate into what it is to believe. We think it strange if, in the civil war which, at this time, disorders our state, we see events float and vary aller a common and ordinary manner; which is because we bring nothing to it but our own. Justice, which is in one party, is only there for ornament and palliation; it, is, indeed, pretended, but 'tis not there received, settled and espoused: it is there, as in the mouth of an advocate, not as in the heart and affection of the party. God owes his extraordinary assistance to faith and religion; not to our passions. Men there are the conductors, and therein serve themselves with religion, whereas it ought to be quite contrary. Observe, if it be not by our own hands that we guide and train it, and draw it like wax into so many contrary figures, from a rule in itself so direct and firm. When and where was this more manifest than in France in our days? They who have taken it on the left hand, they who have taken it on the right; they who call it black, they who call it white, alike employ it to their violent and ambitious designs, conduct it with a progress, so conform in riot and injustice that they render the diversity they pretended in their opinions, in a thing whereon the conduct and rule of our life depends, doubtful and hard to believe. Did one ever see, come from the same school and discipline, manners more united, and more the same? Do but observe with what horrid impudence we toss divine arguments to and fro, and how irreligiously we have both rejected and retaken them, accord—as fortune has shifted our places in these intestine storms.

This so solemn proposition, "Whether it be lawful for a subject to rebel and take up arms against his prince for the defence of his religion," do you remember in whose mouths, the last year, the affirmative of it was the prop of one party, and the negative the pillar of another? And hearken now from what quarter comes the voice and instruction of the one and the other, and if arms make less noise and rattle for this cause than for that. We condemn those to the fire who say that truth must be made to bear the yoke of our necessity; and how much worse does France than say it? Let us confess the truth; whoever should draw out from the army, even that raised by the king, those who take up arms out of pure zeal to religion, and also those who only do it to protect the laws of their country, or for the service of their prince, could hardly, out of both these put together, make one complete company of gens-d'armes. Whence does this proceed, that there are so few to be found who have maintained the same will and the same progress in our civil commotions, and that we see them one while move but a foot-pace, and another run full speed? and the same men one while damage our affairs by their violent heat and fierceness, and another by their coldness, gentleness, and slowness; but that they are pushed on by particular and casual considerations, according to the variety wherein they move?

I evidently perceive that we do not willingly afford devotion any other offices but those that least suit with our own passions.

There hostility so admirable as the Christian. Our zeal performs wonders, when it seconds our inclinations to hatred, cruelty, ambition, avarice, detraction, and rebellion: but when it moves, against the hair, towards bounty, benignity, and temperance, unless, by miracle, some rare and virtuous disposition prompts us to it, we stir neither hand nor toot. Our religion is intended to extirpate vices, whereas it screens, nourishes, and incites them. We must not mock God. If we believed in him, I do not say by faith, but with a simple belief, that is to say (and I speak it to our great shame) if we believed in him and recognised him as we do any other history, or as we would do one of our companions, we should love him above all other things for the infinite bounty and beauty that shines in him;—at least, he would go equal in our affection with riches, pleasure, glory, and our friends. The best of us is not so much afraid to outrage him as he is afraid to injure his neighbour, his kinsman, or his master. Is there any understanding so weak that, having on one side the object of one of our vicious pleasures, and on the other (in equal knowledge and persuasion) the state of an immortal glory, would change the first for the other? and yet we often renounce this out of mere contempt: for what lust tempts us to blaspheme, if not, perhaps, the very desire to offend. The philosopher Antisthenes, as he was being initiated in the mysteries of Orpheus, the priest telling him, "That those who professed themselves of that religion were certain to receive perfect and eternal felicity after death,"—"If thou believest that," answered he, "why dost thou not die thyself?" Diogenes, more rudely, according to his manner, and more remote from our purpose, to the priest that in like manner preached to him, "To become of his religion, that he might obtain the happiness of the other world;—"What!" said he, "thou wouldest have me to believe that Agesilaus and Epaminondas, who were so great men, shall be miserable, and that thou, who art but a calf, and canst do nothing to purpose, shalt be happy, because thou art a priest?" Did we receive these great promises of eternal beatitude with the same reverence and respect that we do a philosophical discourse, we should not have death in so great horror:

Non jam se moriens dissolvi conqurreretur;

Sed magis ire foras, stemque relinquere ut angais,

Gauderet, prealonga senex aut cornua cervus.

"We should not on a death bed grieve to be

Dissolved, but rather launch out cheerfully

From our old hut, and with the snake, be glad

To cast off the corrupted slough we had;

Or with th' old stag rejoice to be now clear

From the large horns, too ponderous grown to bear."

"I desire to be dissolved," we should say, "and to be with Jesus Christ" The force of Plato's arguments concerning the immortality of the soul set some of his disciples to seek a premature grave, that they might the sooner enjoy the things he had made them hope for.

All this is a most evident sign that we only receive our religion after our own fashion, by our own hands, and no otherwise than as other religions are received. Either we are happened in the country where it is in practice, or we reverence the antiquity of it, or the authority of the men who have maintained it, or fear the menaces it fulminates against misbelievers, or are allured by its promises. These considerations ought, 'tis true, to be applied to our belief but as subsidiaries only, for they are human obligations. Another religion, other witnesses, the like promises and threats, might, by the same way, imprint a quite contrary belief. We are Christians by the same title that we are Perigordians or Germans. And what Plato says, "That there are few men so obstinate in their atheism whom a pressing danger will not reduce to an acknowledgment of the divine power," does not concern a true Christian: 'tis for mortal and human religions to be received by human recommendation. What kind of faith can that be that cowardice and want of courage establish in us? A pleasant faith, that does not believe what it believes but for want of courage to disbelieve it! Can a vicious passion, such as inconstancy and astonishment, cause any regular product in our souls? "They are confident in their judgment," says he, "that what is said of hell and future torments is all feigned: but an occasion of making the expedient presenting itself, when old age or diseases bring them to the brink of the grave, the terror of death, by the horror of that future condition, inspires them with a new belief!" And by reason that such impressions render them timorous, he forbids in his Laws all such threatening doctrines, and all persuasion that anything of ill can befall a man from the gods, excepting for his great good when they happen to him, and for a medicinal effect. They say of Bion that, infected with the atheism of Theodoras, he had long had religious men in great scorn and contempt, but that death surprising him, he gave himself up to the most extreme superstition; as if the gods withdrew and returned according to the necessities of Bion. Plato and these examples would conclude that we are brought to a belief of God either by reason or by force. Atheism being a proposition as unnatural as monstrous, difficult also and hard to establish in the human understanding, how arrogant soever, there are men enough seen, out of vanity and pride, to be the authors of extraordinary and reforming opinions, and outwardly to affect the profession of them; who, if they are such fools, have, nevertheless, not the power to plant them in their own conscience. Yet will they not fail to lift up their hands towards heaven if you give them a good thrust with a sword in the breast, and when fear or sickness has abated and dulled the licentious fury of this giddy humour they will easily re-unite, and very discreetly suffer themselves to be reconciled to the public faith and examples. A doctrine seriously digested is one thing, and those superficial impressions another; which springing from the disorder of an unhinged understanding, float at random and great uncertainty in the fancy. Miserable and senseless men, who strive to be worse than they can!

The error of paganism and the ignorance of our sacred truth, let this great soul of Plato, but great only in human greatness, fall also into this other mistake, "That children and old men were most susceptible of religion," as if it sprung and derived its credit from our weakness. The knot that ought to bind the judgment and the will, that ought to restrain the soul and join it to our creator, should be a knot that derives its foldings and strength not from our considerations, from our reasons and passions, but from a divine and supernatural constraint, having but one form, one face, and one lustre, which is the authority of God and his divine grace. Now the heart and soul being governed and commanded by faith, 'tis but reason that they should muster all our other faculties, according as they are able to perform to the service and assistance of their design. Neither is it to be imagined that all this machine has not some marks imprinted upon it by the hand of the mighty architect, and that there is not in the things of this world some image that in some measure resembles the workman who has built and formed them. He has, in his stupendous works, left the character of his divinity, and 'tis our own weakness only that hinders us from discerning it. 'Tis what he himself is pleased to tell us, "That he manifests his invisible operations to us by those that are visible." Sebond applied himself to this laudable and noble study, and demonstrates to us that there is not any part or member of the world that disclaims or derogates from its maker. It were to do wrong to the divine goodness, did not the universe consent to our belief. The heavens, the earth, the elements, our bodies and our souls,—all things concur to this; we have but to find out the way to use them; they instruct us, if we are capable of instruction. For this world is a sacred temple, into which man is introduced, there to contemplate statues, not the works of a mortal hand, but such as the divine purpose has made the objects of sense; the sun, the stars, the water, and the earth, to represent those that are intelligible to us. "The invisible tilings of God," says St. Paul, "appear by the creation of the world, his eternal wisdom and divinity being considered by his works."

> And God himself envies not men the grace
>
> Of seeing and admiring heaven's face;
>
> But, rolling it about, he still anew
>
> Presents its varied splendour to our view,
>
> And on oar minds himself inculcates, so
>
> That we th' Almighty mover well may know:
>
> Instructing us by seeing him the cause
>
> Of ill, to revcreoce and obey his laws."

Now our prayers and human discourses are but as sterile and undigested matter. The grace of God is the form; 'tis that which gives fashion and value to it. As the virtuous actions of Socrates and Cato remain vain and fruitless, for not having had the love and obedience to the true creator of all things, so is it with our imaginations and discourses; they have a kind of body, but it is an inform mass, without fashion and without light, if faith and grace be not added thereto. Faith coming to tinct and illustrate Sehond's arguments renders them firm and stolid; and to that degree that they are capable of serving for directions, and of being the first guides to an elementary Christian to put him into the way of this knowledge. They in some measure form him to, and render him capable of, the grace of God, by which means he afterwards completes and perfects himself in the true belief. I know a man of authority, bred up to letters, who has confessed to me to have been brought back from the errors of unbelief by Sebond's arguments. And should they be stripped of this ornament, and of the assistance and approbation of the faith, and be looked upon as mere fancies only, to contend with those who are precipitated into the dreadful and horrible darkness of irrligion, they will even there find them as solid and firm as any others of the same quality that can be opposed against them; so that we shall be ready to say to our opponents:

Si melius quid habes, arcesse; vel imperium fer:

"If you have arguments more fit.

Produce them, or to these submit."

let them admit the force of our reasons, or let them show us others, and upon some other subject, better woven and of finer thread. I am, unawares, half engaged in the second objection, to which I proposed to make answer in the behalf of Sebond. Some say that his arguments are weak, and unable to make good what he intends, and undertake with great ease to confute them. These are to be a little more roughly handled, for they are more dangerous and malicious than the first Men willingly wrest the sayings of others to favour their own prejudicate opinions. To an atheist all writings tend to atheism: he corrupts the most innocent matter with his own venom. These have their judgments so prepossessed that they cannot relish Sebond's reasons. As to the rest, they think we give them very fair play in putting them into the liberty of combatting our religion with weapons merely human, whom, in her majesty, full of authority and command, they durst not attack. The means that I shall use, and that I think most proper to subdue this frenzy, is to crush and spurn under foot pride and human arrogance; to make them sensible of the inanity, vanity, and vileness of man; to wrest the wretched arms of their reason out of their hands; to make them bow down and bite the ground under the authority and reverence of the Divine Majesty. 'Tis to that alone that knowledge and wisdom appertain; that alone that can make a true estimate of itself, and from which we purloin whatever we value ourselves upon: [—Greek—] "God permits not any being but himself to be truly wise." Let us subdue this presumption, the first foundation of the tyranny of the evil spirit Deus superbis re-sistit, humilibus autem dal gratiam. "God resists the proud, but gives grace to the humble." "Understanding is in the gods," says Plato, "and not at all, or very little, in men." Now it is in the mean time a great consolation to a Christian man to see our frail and mortal parts so fitly suited to our holy and divine faith that, when we employ them to the subjects of their own mortal and frail nature they are not even there more unitedly or more firmly adjusted. Let us see, then, if man has in his power other more forcible and convincing reasons than those of Sebond; that is to say, if it be in him to arrive at any certainty by argument and reason. For St. Augustin, disputing against these people, has good cause to reproach them with injustice, "In that they maintain the part of our belief to be false that our reason cannot establish." And to show that a great many things may be, and have been, of which our nature could not sound the reason and causes, he proposes to them certain known and undoubted experiments, wherein men confess they see nothing; and this he does, as all other things, with a curious and ingenious inquisition. We must do more than this, and make them know that, to convince the weakness of their reason, there is no necessity of culling out uncommon examples: and that it is so defective and so blind that there is no faculty clear enough for it; that to it the easy and the hard are all one; that all subjects equally, and nature in general, disclaim its authority and reject its mediation.

What does truth mean when she preaches to us to fly worldly philosophy, when she so often inculcates to us, "That our wisdom is but folly in the sight of God: that the vainest of all vanities is man: that the man who presumes upon his wisdom does not yet know what wisdom is; and that man, who is nothing, if he thinks himself to be anything, does seduce and deceive himself." These sentences of the Holy Spirit do so clearly and vividly express that which I would maintain that I should need no other proof against men who would with all humility and obedience submit to his authority: but these will be whipped at their own expense, and will not suffer a man to oppose their reason but by itself.

Let us then, for once, consider a man alone, without foreign assistance, armed only with his own proper arms, and unfurnished of the divine grace and wisdom, which is all his honour, strength, and the foundation of his being. Let us see how he stands in this fine equipage. Let him make me understand, by the force of his reason, upon what foundations he has built those great advantages he thinks he has over other creatures. Who has made him believe that this admirable motion of the celestial arch, the eternal light of those luminaries that roll so high over his head, the wondrous and fearful motions of that infinite ocean, should be established and continue so many ages for his service and convenience? Can any thing be imagined so ridiculous, that this miserable and wretched creature, who is not so much as master of himself, but subject to the injuries of all things, should call himself master and emperor of the world, of which he has not power to know the least part, much less to command the whole? And the privilege which he attributes to himself of being the only creature in this vast fabric who has the understanding to discover the beauty and the paris of it; the only one who can return thanks to the architect, and keep account of the revenues and disbursements of the world; who, I wonder, sealed him this patent? Let us see his commission for this great employment Was it granted in favour of the wise only?

Few people will be concerned in it. Are fools and wicked persons worthy so extraordinary a favour, and, being the worst part of the world, to be preferred before the rest? Shall we believe this man?—"For whose sake shall we, therefore, conclude that the world was made? For theirs who have the use of reason: these are gods and men, than whom certainly nothing can be better:" we can never sufficiently decry the impudence of this conjunction. But, wretched creature, what has he in himself worthy of such an advantage? Considering the incorruptible existence of the celestial bodies; beauty; magnitude, and continual revolution by so exact a rule;

    Cum suspicimus mni clestia mundi

Templa super, stellisque micantibus arthera fiium,

El venit in mcntem lun solisque viarurn.

  "When we the heavenly arch above behold.

And the vast sky adorned with stars of gold.

And mark the r'eglar course? that the sun

And moon in their alternate progress run."

considering the dominion and influence those bodies have, not only over our lives and fortunes;

    Facta etenim et vitas hominum suspendit ab aatris;

"Men's lives and actions on the stars depend."

but even over our inclinations, our thoughts and wills, which they govern, incite and agitate at the mercy of their influences, as our reason teaches us;

    "Contemplating the stars he finds that they

Rule by a secret and a silent sway;

And that the enamell'd spheres which roll above

Do ever by alternate causes move.

And, studying these, he can also foresee,

> By certain signs, the turns of destiny;"

seeing that not only a man, not only kings, but that monarchies, empires, and all this lower world follow the influence of the celestial motions,

> "How great a change a little motion brings!
>
> So great this kingdom is that governs kings:"

if our virtue, our vices, our knowledge, and this very discourse we are upon of the power of the stars, and the comparison we are making betwixt them and us, proceed, as our reason supposes, from their favour;

> "One mad in love may cross the raging main,
>
> To level lofty Ilium with the plain;
>
> Another's fate inclines him more by far
>
> To study laws and statutes for the bar.
>
> Sons kill their father, fathers kill their sons,
>
> And one arm'd brother 'gainst another runs..
>
> This war's not their's, but fate's, that spurs them on
>
> To shed the blood which, shed, they must bemoan;
>
> And I ascribe it to the will of fate
>
> That on this theme I now expatiate:"

if we derive this little portion of reason we have from the bounty of heaven, how is it possible that reason should ever make us equal to it? How subject its essence and condition to our knowledge? Whatever we see in those bodies astonishes us: Qu molitio, qua ferramenta, qui vectes, qu machina, qui ministri tanti operis fuerunt? "What contrivance, what tools, what materials, what engines, were employed about so stupendous a work?" Why do we deprive them of soul, of life, and discourse? Have we discovered in them any immoveable or insensible stupidity, we who have no commerce with them but by obedience? Shall we say that we have discovered in no other creature but man the use of a reasonable soul? What! have we seen any thing like the sun? Does he cease to be, because we have seen nothing like him? And do his motions cease, because there are no other like them? If what we have not seen is not, our knowledge is marvellously contracted: Qu sunt tant animi angusti! "How narrow are our understandings!" Are they not dreams of human vanity, to make the moon a celestial earth? there to fancy mountains and vales, as Anaxagoras did? there to fix habitations and human abodes, and plant colonies for our convenience, as Plato and Plutarch have done? And of our earth to make a luminous and resplendent star? "Amongst the other inconveniences of mortality this is one, that darkness of the understanding which leads men astray, not so much from a necessity of erring, but from a love of error. The corruptible body stupifies the soul, and the earthly habitation dulls the faculties of the imagination."

Presumption is our natural and original disease. The most wretched and frail of all creatures is man, and withal the proudest. He feels and sees himself lodged here in the dirt and filth of the world, nailed and rivetted to the worst and deadest part of the universe, in the lowest story of the house, the most remote from the heavenly arch, with animals of the worst condition of the three; and yet in his imagination will be placing himself above the circle of the moon, and bringing the heavens under his feet. 'Tis by the same vanity of imagination that he equals himself to God, attributes to himself divine qualities, withdraws and separates himself from the the crowd of other creatures, cuts out the shares of the animals, his fellows and companions, and distributes to them portions of faculties and force, as himself thinks fit How does he know, by the strength of his understanding, the secret and internal motions of animals?—from what comparison betwixt them and us does he conclude the stupidity he attributes to them? When I play with my cat who knows whether I do not make her more sport than she makes me? We mutually divert one another with our play. If I have my hour to begin or to refus, she also has hers. Plato, in his picture of the golden age under Saturn, reckons, among the chief advantages that a man then had, his communication with beasts, of whom, inquiring and informing himself, he knew the true qualities and differences of them all, by which he acquired a very perfect intelligence and prudence, and led his life more happily than we could do. Need we a better proof to condemn human impudence in the concern of beasts? This great author was of opinion that nature, for the most part in the corporal form she gave them, had only regard to the use of prognostics that were derived thence in his time. The defect that hinders communication betwixt them and us, why may it not be in our part as well as theirs? 'Tis yet to determine where the fault lies that we understand not one another,—for we understand them no more than they do us; and by the same reason they may think us to be beasts as we think them. 'Tis no great wonder if we understand not them, when we do not understand a Basque or a Troglodyte. And yet some have boasted that they understood them, as Apollonius Tyanaus, Melampus, Tiresias, Thales, and others. And seeing, as cusmographers report, that there are nations that have a dog for their king, they must of necessity be able to interpret his voice and motions. We must observe the parity betwixt us, have some tolerable apprehension of their meaning, and so have beasts of ours,—much about the same. They caress us, threaten us, and beg of us, and we do the same to them.

As to the rest, we manifestly discover that they have a full and absolute communication amongst themselves, and that they perfectly understand one another, not only those of the same, but of divers kinds:

"The tamer herds, and wilder sort of brutes.

Though we of higher race conclude them mutes.

Yet utter dissonant and various notes,

From gentler lungs or more distended throats,

As fear, or grief, or anger, do them move,

Or as they do approach the joys of love."

In one kind of barking of a dog the horse knows there is anger, of another sort of bark he is not afraid. Even in the very beasts that have no voice at all, we easily conclude, from the society of offices we obscrvc amongst them, some other sort of communication: their very motions discover it:

"As infants who, for want of words, devise

Expressive motions with their hands and eyes."

And why not, as well as our dumb people, dispute, argue, and tell stories by signs? Of whom I have seen some, by practice, so clever and active that way that, in fact, they wanted nothing of the perfection of making themselves understood. Lovers are angry, reconciled, intreat, thank, appoint, and, in short, speak all things by their eyes:

"Even silence in a lover

Love and passion can discover."

What with the hands? We require, promise, call, dismiss, threaten, pray, supplicate, deny, refuse, interrogate, admire, number, confess, repent, fear, express confusion, doubt, instruct, command, incite, encourage, swear, testify, accuse, condemn, absolve, abuse, despise, defy, provoke, flatter, applaud, bless, submit, mock, reconcile, recommend, exalt, entertain, congratulate, complain, grieve, despair, wonder, exclaim, and what not! And all this with a variety and multiplication, even emulating speech. With the head we invite, remand, confess, deny, give the lie, welcome, honour, reverence, disdain, demand, rejoice, lament, reject, caress, rebuke, submit, huff, encourage, threaten, assure, and inquire. What with the eyebrows?—what with the shoulders! There is not a motion that does not speak, and in an intelligible language without discipline, and a public language that every one understands: whence it should follow, the variety and use distinguished from others considered, that these should rather be judged the property of human nature. I omit what necessity particularly does suddenly suggest to those who are in need;—the alphabets upon the fingers, grammars in gesture, and the sciences which are only by them exercised and expressed; and the nations that Pliny reports have no other language. An ambassador of the city of Abdera, after a long conference with Agis, King of Sparta, demanded of him, "Well, sir, what answer must I return to my fellow-citizens?" "That I have given thee leave," said he, "to say what thou wouldest, and as much as thou wouldest, without ever speaking a word." is not this a silent speaking, and very easy to be understood?

As to the rest, what is there in us that we do not see in the operations of animals? Is there a polity better ordered, the offices better distributed, and more inviolably observed and maintained, than that of bees? Can we imagine that such, and so regular, a distribution of employments can be carried on without reasoning and deliberation?

"Hence to the bee some sages have assign'd

Some portion of the god and heavenly wind."

The swallows that we see at the return of the spring, searching all the corners of our houses for the most commodious places wherein to build their nest; do they seek without judgment, and amongst a thousand choose out the most proper for their purpose, without discretion? And in that elegant and admirable contexture of their buildings, can birds rather make choice of a square figure than a round, of an obtuse than of a right angle, without knowing their properties and effects? Do they bring water, and then clay, without knowing that the hardness of the latter grows softer by being wetted? Do they mat their palace with moss or down without foreseeing that their tender young will lie more safe and easy? Do they secure themselves from the wet and rainy winds, and place their lodgings against the east, without knowing the different qualities of the winds, and considering that one is more wholesome than another? Why does the spider make her web tighter in one place, and slacker in another; why now make one sort of knot, and then another, if she has not deliberation, thought, and conclusion? We sufficiently discover in most of their works how much animals excel us, and how unable our art is to imitate them. We see, nevertheless, in our rougher performances, that we employ all our faculties, and apply the utmost power of our souls; why do we not conclude the same of them?

Why should we attribute to I know not what natural and servile inclination the works that excel all we can do by nature and art? wherein, without being aware, we give them a mighty advantage over us in making nature, with maternal gentleness and love, accompany and learn them, as it were, by the hand to all the actions and commodities of their life, whilst she leaves us to chance and fortune, and to seek out by art the things that are necessary to our conservation, at the same time denying us the means of being able, by any instruction or effort of understanding, to arrive at the natural sufficiency of beasts; so that their brutish stupidity surpasses, in all conveniences, all that our divine intelligence can do. Really, at this rate, we might with great reason call her an unjust stepmother: but it is nothing so, our polity is not so irregular and unformed.

Nature has universally cared for all her creatures, and there is not one she has not amply furnished with all means necessary for the conservation of its being. For the common complaints I hear men make (as the license of their opinions one while lifts them up above the clouds, and then again depresses them to the antipodes), that we are the only animal abandoned naked upon the bare earth, tied and bound, not having wherewithal to arm and clothe us but by the spoil of others; whereas nature has covered all other creatures either with shells, husks, bark, hair, wool, prickles, leather, down, feathers, scales, or silk, according to the necessities of their being; has armed them with talons, teeth, or horns, wherewith to assault and defend, and has herself taught them that which is most proper for them, to swim, to run, to fly, and sing, whereas man neither knows how to walk, speak, eat, or do any thing but weep, without teaching;

"Like to the wretched mariner, when toss'd

By raging seas upon the desert coast,

The tender babe lies naked on the earth,

Of all supports of life stript by his birth;

When nature first presents him to the day,

Freed from the cell wherein before he lay,

He fills the ambient air with doleful cries.

Foretelling thus life's future miseries;

But beasts, both wild and tame, greater and less,

Do of themselves in strength and bulk increase;

They need no rattle, nor the broken chat,

Ay which the nurse first teaches boys to prate

They look not out for different robes to wear,

According to the seasons of the year;

And need no arms nor walls their goods to save,

Since earth and liberal nature ever have,

And will, in all abundance, still produce

All things whereof they can have need or use:"

these complaints are false; there is in the polity of the world a greater equality and more uniform relation. Our skins are as sufficient to defend us from the injuries of the weather as theirs are; witness several nations that yet know not the use of clothes. Our ancient Gauls were but slenderly clad, any more than the Irish, our neighbours, though in so cold a climate; but we may better judge of this by ourselves: for all those parts that we are pleased to expose to the air are found very able to endure it: the face, the feet, the hands, the arms, the head, according to the various habit; if there be a tender part about us, and that would seem to be in danger from cold, it should be the stomach where the digestion is; and yet our forefathers were there always open, and our ladies, as tender and delicate as they are, go sometimes half-bare as low as the navel. Neither is the binding or swathing of infants any more necessary; and the Lacedmoman mothers brought theirs in all liberty of motion of members, without any ligature at all. Our crying is common with the greatest part of other animals, and there are but few creatures that are not observed to groan, and bemoan themselves a long time after they come into the world; forasmuch as it is a behaviour suitable to the weakness wherein they find themselves. As to the custom of eating, it is in us, as in them, natural, and without instruction;

"For every one soon finds his natural force.

Which he, or better may employ, or worse."

Who doubts but an infant, arrived to the strength of feeding himself, may make shift to find something to eat And the earth produces and offers him wherewithal to supply his necessity, without other culture and artifice; and if not at all times, no more does she do it to beasts, witness the provision we see ants and other creatures hoard up against the dead seasons of the year. The late discovered nations, so abundantly furnished with natural meat and drink, without care, or without cookery, may give us to understand that bread is not our only food, and that, without tillage, our mother nature has provided us sufficiently of all we stand in need of: nay, it appears more fully and plentifully than she does at present, now that we have added our own industry:

"The earth did first spontaneously afford

Choice fruits and wines to furnish out the board;

With herbs and flow'rs unsown in verdant fields.

But scarce by art so good a harvest yields;

Though men and oxen mutually have strove,

With all their utmost force the soil t' improve,"

the debauchery and irregularity of our appetites outstrips all the inventions we can contrive to satisfy it.

As to arms, we have more natural ones than than most other animals more various motions of limbs, and naturally and without lesson extract more service from them. Those that are trained to fight naked are seen to throw themselves into the like hazards that we do. If some beasts surpass us in this advantage, we surpass many others. And the industry of fortifying the body, and covering it by acquired means, we have by instinct and natural precept? That it is so, the elephant shows who sharpen, and whets the teeth he makes use of in war (for he has particular ones for that service, which he spares, and never employs them at all to any other use); when bulls go to fight, they toss and throw the dust about them; boars whet their tusks; and the ichneumon, when he is about to engage with the crocodile, fortifies his body, and covers and crusts it all over with close-wrought and well-tempered slime, as with a cuirass. Why shall we not say that it is also natural for us to arm ourselves with wood and iron?

As to speech, it is certain that if it be not natural it is not necessary. Nevertheless I believe that a child which had been brought up in an absolute solitude, remote from all society of men (which would be an experiment very hard to make), would have some kind of speech to express his meaning by. And 'tis not to be supposed that nature should have denied that to us which she has given to several other animals: for what is this faculty we observe in them, of complaining, rejoicing, calling to one another for succour, and inviting each other to love, which they do with the voice, other than speech? And why should they not speak to one another? They speak to us, and we to them. In how many several sorts of ways do we speak to our dogs, and they answer us? We converse with them in another sort of language, and use other appellations, than we do with birds, hogs, oxen, horses, and alter the idiom according to the kind.

"Thus from one swarm of ants some sally out.

To spy another's stock or mark its rout."

Lactantius seems to attribute to beasts not only speech, but laughter also. And the difference of language which is seen amongst us, according to the difference of countries, is also observed in animals of the same kind. Aristotle, in proof of this, instances the Various calls of partridges, according to the situation of places:

"And various birds do from their warbling throats

At various times, utter quite different notes,

And some their hoarse songs with the seasons change."

But it is yet to be known what language this child would speak; and of that what is said by guess has no great appearance. If a man will allege to me, in opposition to this opinion, that those who are naturally deaf speak not, I answer that this is not only because they could not receive the instruction of speaking by ear, but rather because the sense of hearing, of which they are deprived, relates to that of speaking, and that these hold together by a natural and inseparable tie, in such manner that what we speak we must first speak to ourselves within, and make it sound in our own ears, before we can utter it to others.

All this I have said to prove the resemblance there is in human things, and to bring us back and join us to the crowd. We are neither above nor below the rest All that is under heaven, says the sage, runs one law and one fortune:

"All things remain

Bound and entangled in one fatal chain."

There is, indeed, some difference,—there are several orders and degrees; but it is under the aspect of one and the same nature:

"All things by their own rites proceed, and draw

Towards their ends, by nature's certain law."

Man must be compelled and restrained within the bounds of this polity. Miserable creature! he is not in a condition really to step over the rail. He is fettered and circumscribed, he is subjected to the same necessity that the other creatures of his rank and order are, and of a very mean condition, without any prerogative of true and real pre-eminence. That which he attributes to himself, by vain fancy and opinion, has neither body nor taste. And if it be so, that he only, of all the animals, has this liberty of imagination and irregularity of thoughts, representing to him that which is, that which is not, and that he would have, the false and the true, 'tis an advantage dearly bought, and of which he has very little reason to be proud; for thence springs the principal and original fountain of all the evils that befal him,—sin, sickness, irresolution, affliction, despair. I say, then, to return to my subject, that there is no appearance to induce a man to believe that beasts should, by a natural and forced inclination, do the same things that we do by our choice and industry. We ought from like effects to conclude like faculties, and from greater effects greater faculties; and consequently confess that the same reasoning, and the same ways by which we operate, are common with them, or that they have others that are better. Why should we imagine this natural constraint in them, who experience no such effect in ourselves? added that it is more honourable to be guided and obliged to act regularly by a natural and inevitable condition, and nearer allied to the divinity, than to act regularly by a temerarious and fortuitous liberty, and more safe to entrust the reins of our conduct in the hands of nature than our own. The vanity of our presumption makes us prefer rather to owe our sufficiency to our own exertions than to her bounty, and to enrich the other animals with natural goods, and abjure them in their favour, in order to honour and ennoble ourselves with goods acquired, very foolishly in my opinion; for I should as much value parts and virtues naturally and purely my own as those I had begged and obtained from education. It is not in our power to obtain a nobler reputation than to be favoured of God and nature.

For instance, take the fox, the people of Thrace make use of when they wish to pass over the ice of some frozen river, and turn him out before them to that purpose; when we see him lay his ear upon the bank of the river, down to the ice, to listen if from a more remote or nearer distance he can hear the noise of the waters' current, and, according as he finds by that the ice to be of a less or greater thickness, to retire or advance,—have we not reason to believe thence that the same rational thoughts passed through his head that we should have upon the like occasions; and that it is a ratiocination and consequence, drawn from natural sense, that that which makes a noise runs, that which runs is not frozen, what is not frozen is liquid, and that which is liquid yields to impression! For to attribute this to a mere quickness of the sense of hearing, without reason and consequence, is a chimra that cannot enter into the imagination. We are to suppose the same of the many sorts of subtleties and inventions with which beasts secure themselves from, and frustrate, the enterprizes we plot against them.

And if we will make an advantage even of this, that it is in our power to seize them, to employ them in our service, and to use them at our pleasure, 'tis still but the same advantage we have over one another. We have our slaves upon these terms: the Climacid, were they not women in Syria who, squat on all fours, served for a ladder or footstool, by which the ladies mounted their coaches? And the greatest part of free persons surrender, for very trivial conveniences, their life and being into the power of another. The wives and concubines of the Thracians contended who should be chosen to be slain upon their husband's tomb. Have tyrants ever failed of finding men enough vowed to their devotion? some of them moreover adding this necessity, of accompanying them in death as well as life? Whole armies have bound themselves after this manner to their captains. The form of the oath in the rude school of gladiators was in these words: "We swear to suffer ourselves to be chained, burnt, wounded, and killed with the sword, and to endure all that true gladiators suffer from their master, religiously engaging both body and soul in his service."

    Uire meum, si vis, flamma caput, et pete ferro

    Corpus, et iutorto verbere terga seca.

    "Wound me with steel, or burn my head with fire.

    Or scourge my shoulders with well-twisted wire."

This was an obligation indeed, and yet there, in one year, ten thousand entered into it, to their destruction. When the Scythians interred their king they strangled upon his body the most beloved of his concubines, his cup-bearer, the master of his horse, his chamberlain, the usher of his chamber, and his cook. And upon the anniversary thereof they killed fifty horses, mounted by fifty pages, that they had impaled all up the spine of the back to the throat, and there left them fixed in triumph about his tomb. The men that serve us do it cheaper, and for a less careful and favourable usage than what we treat our hawks, horses and dogs withal. To what solicitude do we not submit for the conveniences of these? I do not think that servants of the most abject condition would willingly do that for their masters that princes think it an honour to do for their beasts. Diogenes seeing his relations solicitous to redeem, him from servitude: "They are fools," said he; "'tis he that keeps and nourishes me that in reality serves me." And they who entertain beasts ought rather to be said to serve them, than to be served by them. And withal in this these have something more generous in that one lion never submitted to another lion, nor one horse to another, for want of courage. As we go to the chase of beasts, so do tigers and lions to the chase of men, and do the same execution upon one another; dogs upon hares, pikes upon tench, swallows upon grass-hoppers, and sparrow-hawks upon blackbirds and larks:

"The stork with snakes and lizards from the wood

And pathless wilds supports her callow brood,

While Jove's own eagle, bird of noble blood,

Scours the wide country for undaunted food;

Sweeps the swift hare or swifter fawn away,

And feeds her nestlings with the generous prey."

We divide the quarry, as well as the pains and labour of the chase, with our hawks and hounds. And about Amphipolis, in Thrace, the hawkers and wild falcons equally divide the prey in the half. As also along the lake Motis, if the fisherman does not honestly leave the wolves an equal share of what he has caught, they presently go and tear his nets in pieces. And as we have a way of sporting that is carried on more by subtlety than force, as springing hares, and angling with line and hook, there is also the like amongst other animals. Aristotle says that the cuttle-fish casts a gut out of her throat as long as a line, which she extends and draws back at pleasure; and as she perceives some little fish approach her she lets it nibble upon the end of this gut, lying herself concealed in the sand or mud, and by little and little draws it in, till the little fish is so near her that at one spring she may catch it.

As to strength, there is no creature in the world exposed to so many injuries as man. We need not a whale, elephant, or a crocodile, nor any such-like animals, of which one alone is sufficient to dispatch a great number of men, to do our business; lice are sufficient to vacate Sylla's dictatorship; and the heart and life of a great and triumphant emperor is the breakfast of a little contemptible worm!

Why should we say that it is only for man, or knowledge built up by art and meditation, to distinguish the things useful for his being, and proper for the cure of his diseases, and those which are not; to know the virtues of rhubarb and polypody. When we see the goats of Candia, when wounded with an arrow, among a million of plants choose out dittany for their cure; and the tortoise, when she has eaten a viper, immediately go out to look for origanum to purge her; the dragon to rub and clear his eyes with fennel; the storks to give themselves clysters of sea-water; the elephants to draw not only out of their own bodies, and those of their companions, but out of the bodies of their masters too (witness the elephant of King Porus whom Alexander defeated), the darts and javelins thrown at them in battle, and that so dexterously that we ourselves could not do it with so little pain to the patient;—why do we not say here also that this is knowledge and reason? For to allege, to their disparagement, that 'tis by the sole instruction and dictate of nature that they know all this, is not to take from them the dignity of knowledge and reason, but with greater force to attribute it to them than to us, for the honour of so infallible a mistress. Chrysippus, though in other things as scornful a judge of the condition of animals as any other philosopher whatever, considering the motions of a dog, who coming to a place where three ways met, either to hunt after his master he has lost, or in pursuit of some game that flies before him, goes snuffing first in one of the ways, and then in another, and, after having made himself sure of two, without finding the trace of what he seeks, dashes into the third without examination, is forced to confess that this reasoning is in the dog: "I have traced my master to this place; he must of necessity be gone one of these three ways; he is not gone this way nor that, he must then infallibly be gone this other;" and that assuring himself by this conclusion, he makes no use of his nose in the third way, nor ever lays it to the ground, but suffers himself to be carried on there by the force of reason. This sally, purely logical, and this use of propositions divided and conjoined, and the right enumeration of parts, is it not every whit as good that the dog knows all this of himself as well as from Trapezuntius?

Animals are not incapable, however, of being instructed after our method. We teach blackbirds, ravens, pies, and parrots, to speak: and the facility wherewith we see they lend us their voices, and render both them and their breath so supple and pliant, to be formed and confined within a certain number of letters and syllables, does evince that they have a reason within, which renders them so docile and willing to learn. Everybody, I believe, is glutted with the several sorts of tricks that tumblers teach their dogs; the dances, where they do not miss any one cadence of the sound they hear; the several various motions and leaps they make them perform by the command of a word. But I observe this effect with the greatest admiration, which nevertheless is very common, in the dogs that lead the blind, both in the country and in cities: I have taken notice how they stop at certain doors, where they are wont to receive alms; how they avoid the encounter of coaches and carts, even there where they have sufficient room to pass; I have seen them, by the trench of a town, forsake a plain and even path and take a worse, only to keep their masters further from the ditch;—how could a man have made this dog understand that it was his office to look to his master's safely only, and to despise his own conveniency to serve him? And how had he the knowledge that a way was wide enough for him that was not so for a blind man? Can all this be apprehended without ratiocination!

I must not omit what Plutarch says he saw of a dog at Rome with the Emperor Vespasian, the father, at the theatre of Marcellus. This dog served a player, that played a farce of several parts and personages, and had therein his part. He had, amongst other things, to counterfeit himself for some time dead, by reason of a certain drug he was supposed to eat After he had swallowed a piece of bread, which passed for the drug, he began after awhile to tremble and stagger, as if he was taken giddy: at last, stretching himself out stiff, as if dead, he suffered himself to be drawn and dragged from place to place, as it was his part to do; and afterward, when he knew it to be time, he began first gently to stir, as if awaking out of a profound sleep, and lifting up his head looked about him after such a manner as astonished all the spectators.

The oxen that served in the royal gardens of Susa, to water them, and turn certain great wheels to draw water for that purpose, to which buckets were fastened (such as there are many in Languedoc), being ordered every one to draw a hundred turns a day, they were so accustomed to this number that it was impossible by any force to make them draw one turn more; but, their task being performed, they would suddenly stop and stand still. We are almost men before we can count a hundred, and have lately discovered nations that have no knowledge of numbers at all.

There is more understanding required in the teaching of others than in being taught. Now, setting aside what Democritus held and proved, "That most of the arts we have were taught us by other animals," as by the spider to weave and sew; by the swallow to build; by the swan and nightingale music; and by several animals to make medicines:—Aristotle is of opinion "That the nightingales teach their young ones to sing, and spend a great deal of time and care in it;" whence it happens that those we bring up in cages, and which have not had the time to learn of their parents, want much of the grace of their singing: we may judge by this that they improve by discipline and study; and, even amongst the wild, it is not all and every one alike—every one has learnt to do better or worse, according to their capacity. And so jealous are they one of another, whilst learning, that they contention with emulation, and by so vigorous a contention that sometimes the vanquished fall dead upon the place, the breath rather failing than the voice. The younger ruminate pensively and begin to mutter some broken notes; the disciple listens to the master's lesson, and gives the best account he is able; they are silent oy turns; one may hear faults corrected and observe some reprehensions of the teacher. " have formerly seen," says Arrian, "an elephant having a cymbal hung at each leg, and another fastened to his trunk, at the sound of which all the others danced round about him, rising and bending at certain cadences, as they were guided by the instrument; and 'twas delightful to hear this harmony." In the spectacles of Rome there were ordinarily seen elephants taught to move and dance to the sound of the voice, dances wherein were several changes and cadences very hard to learn. And some have been known so intent upon their lesson as privately to practice it by themselves, that they might not be chidden nor beaten by their masters.

But this other story of the pie, of which we have Plutarch himself for a warrant, is very strange. She lived in a barber's shop at Rome, and did wonders in imitating with her voice whatever she heard. It happened one day that certain trumpeters stood a good while sounding before the shop. After that, and all the next day, the pie was pensive, dumb, and melancholic; which every body wondered at, and thought the noise of the trumpets had so stupified and astonished her that her voice was gone with her hearing. But they found at last that it was a profound meditation and a retiring into herself, her thoughts exercising and preparing her voice to imitate the sound of those trumpets, so that the first voice she uttered was perfectly to imitate their strains, stops, and changes; having by this new lesson quitted and taken in disdain all she had learned before.

I will not omit this other example of a dog, also, which the same Plutarch (I am sadly confounding all order, but I do not propose arrangement here any more than elsewhere throughout my book) which Plutarch says he saw on board a ship. This dog being puzzled how to get the oil that was in the bottom of a jar, which he could not reach with his tongue by reason of the narrow mouth of the vessel, went and fetched stones and let them fall into the jar till he made the oil rise so high that he could reach it. What is this but an effect of a very subtle capacity! 'Tis said that the ravens of Barbary do the same, when the water they would drink is too low. This action is somewhat akin to what Juba, a king of their nation relates of the elephants: "That when, by the craft of the hunter, one of them is trapped in certain deep pits prepared for them, and covered over with brush to deceive them, all the rest, in great diligence, bring a great many stones and logs of wood to raise the bottom so that he may get out." But this animal, in several other effects, comes so near to human capacity that, should I particularly relate all that experience hath delivered to us, I should easily have what I usually maintain granted: namely, that there is more difference betwixt such and such a man than betwixt such a beast and such a man. The keeper of an elephant in a private house of Syria robbed him every meal of the half of his allowance. One day his master would himself feed him, and poured the full measure of barley he had ordered for his allowance into his manger which the elephant, casting an angry look at the keeper, with his trunk separated the one-half from the other, and thrust it aside, by that declaring the wrong was done him. And another, having a keeper that mixed stones with his corn to make up the measure, came to the pot where he was boiling meat for his own dinner, and filled it with ashes. These are particular effects: but that which all the world has seen, and all the world knows, that in all the armies of the Levant one of the greatest force consisted in elephants, with whom they did, without comparison, much greater execution than we now do with our artillery; which takes, pretty nearly, their place in a day of battle (as may easily be supposed by such as are well read in ancient history);

"The sires of these huge animals were wont

The Carthaginian Hannibal to mount;

Our leaders also did these beasts bestride,

And mounted thus Pyrrhus his foes defied;

Nay, more, upon their backs they used to bear

Castles with armed cohorts to the war."

They must necessarily have very confidently relied upon the fidelity and understanding of these beasts when they entrusted them with the vanguard of a battle, where the least stop they should have made, by reason of the bulk and heaviness of their bodies, and the least fright that should have made them face about upon their own people, had been enough to spoil all: and there are but few examples where it has happened that they have fallen foul upon their own troops, whereas we ourselves break into our own battalions and rout one another. They had the charge not of one simple movement only, but of many several things to be performed in the battle: as the Spaniards did to their dogs in their new conquest of the Indies, to whom they gave pay and allowed them a share in the spoil; and those animals showed as much dexterity and judgment in pursuing the victory and stopping the pursuit; in charging and retiring, as occasion required; and in distinguishing their friends from their enemies, as they did ardour and fierceness.

We more admire and value things that are unusual and strange than those of ordinary observation. I had not else so long insisted upon these examples: for I believe whoever shall strictly observe what we ordinarily see in those animals we have amongst us may there find as wonderful effects as those we seek in remote countries and ages. 'Tis one and the same nature that rolls on her course, and whoever has sufficiently considered the present state of things, might certainly conclude as to both the future ana the past. I have formerly seen men, brought hither by sea from very distant countries, whose language not being understood by us, and moreover their mien, countenance, and habit, being quite differing from ours; which of us did not repute them savages and brutes! Who did not attribute it to stupidity and want of common sense to see them mute, ignorant of the French tongue, ignorant of our salutations and cringes, our port and behaviour, from which all human nature must by all means take its pattern and example. All that seems strange to us, and that we do not understand, we condemn. The same thing happens also in the judgments we make of beasts. They have several conditions like to ours; from those we may, by comparison, draw some conjecture: but by those qualities that are particular to themselves, what know we what to make of them! The horses, dogs, oxen, sheep, birds, and most of the animals that live amongst us, know our voices, and suffer themselves to be governed by them: so did Crassus's lamprey, and came when he called it; as also do the eels that are found in the Lake Arethusa; and I have seen several ponds where the fishes come to eat at a certain call of those who use to feed them.

> "They every one have names, and one and all
>
> Straightway appear at their own master's call:"

We may judge of that. We may also say that the elephants have some participation of religion forasmuch as after several washings and purifications they are observed to lift up their trunk like arms, and, fixing their eyes towards the rising of the sun, continue long in meditation and contemplation, at certain hours of the days, of their own motion; without instruction or precept But because we do not see any such signs in other animals, we cannot for that conclude that they are without religion, nor make any judgment of what is concealed from us. As we discern something in this action which the philosopher Cleanthes took notice of, because it something resembles our own. He saw, he says, "Ants go from their ant-hill, carrying the dead body of an ant towards another ant-hill, whence several other ants came out to meet them, as if to speak with them; where, after having been a while together, the last returned to consult, you may suppose, with their fellow-citizens, and so made two or three journeys, by reason of the difficulty of capitulation. In the conclusion, the last comers brought the first a worm out of their burrow, as it were for the ransom of the defunct, which the first laid upon their backs and carried home, leaving the dead body to the others." This was the interpretation that Cleanthes gave of this transaction, giving us by that to understand that those creatures that have no voice are not, nevertheless, without intercourse and mutual communication, whereof 'tis through our own defect that we do not participate; and for that reason foolishly take upon us to pass our censure. But they yet produce either effects far beyond our capacity, to which we are so far from being able to arrive by imitation that we cannot so much as by imitation conceive it. Many are of opinion that in the great and last naval engagement that Antony lost to Augustus, his admiral galley was stayed in the middle of her course by the little fish the Latins call remora, by reason of the property she has of staying all sorts of vessels to which she fastens herself. And the Emperor Caligula, sailing with a great navy upon the coast of Romania, his galley only was suddenly stayed by the same fish, which, he caused to be taken, fastened as it was to the keel of his ship, very angry that such a little animal could resist both the sea, the wind, and the force of all his oars, by being only fastened by the beak to his galley (for it is a shell-fish); and was moreover, not without great reason, astonished that, being brought to him in the vessel, it had no longer the strength it had without. A citizen of Cyzicus formerly acquired the reputation of a good mathematician for having learnt the quality of the hedge-hog: he has his burrow open in divers places, and to several winds, and, foreseeing the wind that is to come, stops the hole on that side, which that citizen observing, gave the city certain predictions of the wind which was presently to blow. The camlon takes her colour from the place upon which she is laid; but the polypus gives himself what colour he pleases, according to occasion, either to conceal himself from what he fears, or from what he has a design to seize: in the camlon 'tis a passive, but in the polypus 'tis an active, change. We have some changes of colour, as in fear, anger, shame, and other passions, that alter our complexions; but it is by the effect of suffering, as with the camlon. It is in the power of the jaundice, indeed, to make us turn yellow, but 'tis not in the power of our own will. Now these effects that we discover in other animals, much greater than ours, seem to imply some more excellent faculty in them unknown to us; as 'tis to be presumed there are several other qualities and abilities of theirs, of which no appearances have arrived at us.

Amongst all the predictions of elder times, the most ancient and the most certain were those taken from the flight of birds; we have nothing certain like it, nor any thing to be so much admired. That rule and order of the moving of the wing, whence they derived the consequences of future things, must of necessity be guided by some excellent means to so noble an operation: for to attribute this great effect to any natural disposition, without the intelligence, consent, and meditation of him by whom it is produced, is an opinion evidently false. That it is so, the cramp-fish has this quality, not only to benumb all the members that touch her, but even through the nets transmit a heavy dulness into the hands of those that move and handle them; nay, it is further said that if one pour water upon her, he will feel this numbness mount up the water to the hand, and stupefy the feeling through the water. This is a miraculous force; but 'tis not useless to the cramp-fish; she knows it, and makes use on't; for, to catch the prey she desires, she will bury herself in the mud, that other fishes swimming over her, struck and benumbed with this coldness of hers, may fall into her power. Cranes, swallows, and other birds of passage, by shifting their abode according to the seasons, sufficiently manifest the knowledge they have of their divining faculty, and put it in use. Huntsmen assure us that to cull out from amongst a great many puppies that which ought to be preserved as the best, the best way is to refer the choice to the mother; as thus, take them and carry them out of the kennel, and the first she brings back will certainly be the best; or if you make a show as if you would environ the kennel with fire, that one she first catches up to save. By which it appears they have a sort of prognostic which we have not; or that they have some virtue in judging of their whelps other and more certain than we have.

The manner of coming into the world, of engendering, nourishing, acting, moving, living and dying of beasts, is so near to ours that whatever we retrench from their moving causes, and add to our own condition above theirs, can by no means proceed from any meditation of our own reason. For the regimen of our health, physicians propose to us the example of the beasts' manners and way of living; for this saying (out of Plutarch) has in all times been in the mouth of these people: "Keep warm thy feet and head, as to the rest, live like a beast."

The chief of all natural actions is generation; we have a certain disposition of members which is the most proper for us to that end; nevertheless, we are ordered by Lucretius to conform to the gesture and posture of the brutes as the most effectual:—

  More ferarum,

  Quadrupedumque magis ritu, plerumque putantur

  Concipere uxores:

  Quia sic loca sumere possunt,

Pectoribus positis, sublatis semina lumbis;

and the same authority condemns, as hurtful, those indiscreet and impudent motions which the women have added of their own invention, to whom it proposes the more temperate and modest pattern and practice of the beasts of their own sex:—

Nam mulier prohibet se concipere atque rpugnt,

Clunibus ipsa viri Venerem si Ita retractet,

Atque exossato ciet omni pectore fluctua.

Ejicit enim sulci recta regione viaque

Vomerem, atque locis avertit seminis ictum.

If it be justice to render to every one their due, the beasts that serve, love, and defend their benefactors, and that pursue and fall upon strangers and those who offend them, do in this represent a certain air of our justice; as also in observing a very equitable equality in the distribution of what they have to their young. And as to friendship, they have it without comparison more lively and constant than men have. King Lysimachus's dog, Hyrcanus, master being dead, lay on his bed, obstinately refusing either to eat or drink; and, the day that his body was burnt, he took a run and leaped into the fire, where he was consumed, As also did the dog of one Pyrrhus, for he would not stir from off his master's bed from the time he died; and when they carried him away let himself be carried with him, and at last leaped into the pile where they burnt his master's body. There are inclinations of affection which sometimes spring in us, without the consultation of reason; and by a fortuitous temerity, which others call sympathy; of which beasts are as capable as we. We see horses take such an acquaintance with one another that we have much ado to make them eat or travel, when separated; we observe them to fancy a particular colour in those of their own kind, and, where they meet it, run to it with great joy and demonstrations of good will, and have a dislike and hatred for some other colour. Animals have choice, as well as we, in their amours, and cull out their mistresses; neither are they exempt from our jealousies and implacable malice.

Desires are either natural and necessary, as to eat and drink; or natural and not necessary, as the coupling with females; or neither natural nor necessary; of which last sort are almost all the desires of men; they are all superfluous and artificial. For 'tis marvellous how little will satisfy nature, how little she has left us to desire; our ragouts and kickshaws are not of her ordering. The Stoics say that a man may live on an olive a day. The delicacy of our wines is no part of her instruction, nor the refinements we introduce into the indulgence of our amorous appetites:—

Neque ilia

Magno prognatum deposcit consule cunnum.

"Nature, in her pursuit of love, disclaims

The pride of titles, and the pomp of names."

These irregular desires, that the ignorance of good and a false opinion have infused into us, are so many that they almost exclude all the natural; just as if there were so great a number of strangers in the city as to thrust out the natural inhabitants, or, usurping upon their ancient rights and privileges, should extinguish their authority and introduce new laws and customs of their own. Animals are much more regular than we, and keep themselves with greater moderation within the limits nature has prescribed; but yet not so exactly that they have not sometimes an analogy with our debauches. And as there have been furious desires that have impelled men to the love of beasts, so there have been examples of beasts that have fallen in love with us, and been seized with monstrous affection betwixt kinds; witness the elephant who was rival to Aristophanes the grammarian in the love of a young herb-wench in the city of Alexandria, who was nothing behind him in all the offices of a very passionate suitor; for going through the market where they sold fruit, he would take some in his trunk and carry them to her. He would as much as possible keep her always in his sight, and would sometimes put his trunk under her handkerchief into her bosom, to feel her breasts. They tell also of a dragon in love with a girl, and of a goose enamoured of a child; of a ram that was suitor to the minstrelless Glaucia, in the town of Asopus; and we see not unfrequently baboons furiously in love with women. We see also certain male animals that are fond of the males of their own kind. Oppian and others give us some examples of the reverence that beasts have to their kindred in their copulations; but experience often shows us the contrary:—

Nec habetur turpe juvenc

Ferre patrem tergo; fit equo sua filia conjux;

Quasque creavit, init pecudes caper; ipsaque cujus

Semine concepta est, ex illo concipit ales.

"The heifer thinks it not a shame to take

Her lusty sire upon her willing back:

The horse his daughter leaps, goats scruple not

T' increase the herd by those they have begot;

And birds of all sorts do in common live,

And by the seed they have conceived conceive."

And for subtle cunning, can there be a more pregnant example than in the philosopher Thales's mule? who, fording a river, laden with salt, and by accident stumbling there, so that the sacks he carried were all wet, perceiving that by the melting of the salt his burden was something lighter, he never failed, so oft as he came to any river, to lie down with his load; till his master, discovering the knavery, ordered that he should be laden with wood? wherein, finding himself mistaken, he ceased to practise that device. There are several that very vividly represent the true image of our avarice; for we see them infinitely solicitus to get all they can, and hide it with that exceeding great care, though they never make any use of it at all. As to thrift, they surpass us not only in the foresight and laying up, and saving for the time to come, but they have, moreover, a great deal of the science necessary thereto. The ants bring abroad into the sun their grain and seed to air, refresh and dry them when they perceive them to mould and grow musty, lest they should decay and rot. But the caution and prevention they use in gnawing their grains of wheat surpass all imagination of human prudence; for by reason that the wheat does not always continue sound and dry, but grows soft, thaws and dissolves as if it were steeped in milk, whilst hasting to germination; for fear lest it should shoot and lose the nature and property of a magazine for their subsistence, they nibble off the end by which it should shoot and sprout.

As to what concerns war, which is the greatest and most magnificent of human actions, I would very fain know whether we would use it for an argument of some prerogative or, on contrary, for a testimony of our weakness and imperfection; as, in truth, the science of undoing and killing one another, and of ruining and destroying our own kind, has nothing in it so tempting as to make it be coveted by beasts who have it not.

> Quando leoni Fortior eripuit vitam leo? quo nemore unquam
>
> Expiravit aper majoris dentibus apri?

> "No lion drinks a weaker lion's gore,
>
> No boar expires beneath a stronger boar."

Yet are they not universally exempt; witness the furious encounters of bees, and the enterprises of the princes of the contrary armies:—

> Spe duobus Regibus incessit magno discordia motu;
>
> Continuoque animos vulgi et trepidantia bello
>
> Gorda licet long prsciscere.

"But if contending factions arm the hive,

When rival kings in doubtful battle strive,

Tumultuous crowds the dread event prepare,

And palpitating hearts that beat to war."

I never read this divine description but that, methinks, I there see human folly and vanity represented in their true and lively colours. For these warlike movements, that so ravish us with their astounding noise and horror, this rattle of guns, drums, and cries,

Fulgur ibi ad coelum se tollit, totaque circum

re renidescit tellus, subterque virm vi

Excitur pedibus sonitus, clamoreque montes

Icti rejectant voces ad sidera mundi;

"When burnish'd arms to heaven dart their rays,

And many a steely beam i' th' sunlight plays,

When trampled is the earth by horse and man,

Until the very centre groans again,

And that the rocks, struck by the various cries,

Reverberate the sound unto the skies;"

in the dreadful embattling of so many thousands of armed men, and so great fury, ardour, and courage, 'tis pleasant to consider by what idle occasions they are excited, and by how light ones appeased:—

Paridis propter narratur amorem

Greci Barbari diro collisa duello:

"Of wanton Paris the illicit love

Did Greece and Troy to ten years' warfare move:"

all Asia was ruined and destroyed for the lust of Paris; the envy of one single man, a despite, a pleasure, a domestic jealousy, causes that ought not to set two oyster-wenches by the ears, is the mover of all this mighty bustle. Shall we believe those very men who are themselves the principal authors of these mischiefs? Let us then hear the greatest, the most powerful, the most victorious emperor that ever was, turning into a jest, very pleasantly and ingeniously, several battles fought both by sea and land, the blood and lives of five hundred thousand men that followed his fortune, and the strength and riches of two parts of the world drained for the expense of his expeditions:—

Quod futuit Glaphyran Antonius, hanc mihi poenam

Fulvia constituit, se quoqne uti futuam.

Fulviam ego ut futuam! quid, si me Manius oret

Podicem, faciam? Non puto, si sapiam.

Aut futue, aut pugnemus, ait

Quid, si mihi vitii

Charior est ips mentula? Signa canant.

Qui? moi, que je serve Fulvie!

Sufflt-il quelle en ait envie?

A ce compte, on verrait se retirer von moi

Mille pouses mal satisfaites.

Aime-moi, me dit elle, ou combattons. Mais quoi?

Elle est bien laide! Allons, sonnes trompettes.

'Cause Anthony is fired with Glaphire's charms

Fain would his Fulvia tempt me to her arms.

If Anthony be false, what then? must I

Be slave to Fulvia's lustful tyranny?

Then would a thousand wanton, waspish wives,

(I use my Latin with the liberty of conscience you are pleased to allow me.) Now this great body, with so many fronts, and so many motions, which seems to threaten heaven and earth:—

Quam multi Lybico volvuntur marmore fluctus,

Svus ubi Orion hibemis conditur undis,

Vel quam solo novo dens torrentur Arist,

Aut Hermi campo, aut Lyci flaventibus arvis;

Scuta sonant, pulsuque pedum tremit excita tellus:

"Not thicker billows beat the Lybian main,

When pale Orion sits in wintry rain;

Nor thicker harvests on rich Hermus rise,

Or Lycian fields, when Phobus burns the skies,

Than stand these troops: their bucklers ring around;

Their trampling turns the turf and shakes the solid ground:"

this furious monster, with so many heads and arms, is yet man—feeble, calamitous, and miserable man! 'Tis but an ant-hill disturbed and provoked:—

It nigrum campis agmen:

"The black troop marches to the field:"

a contrary blast, the croaking of a flight of ravens, the stumble of a horse, the casual passage of an eagle, a dream, a voice, a sign, a morning mist, are any one of them sufficient to beat down and overturn him. Dart but a sunbeam in his face, he is melted and vanished. Blow but a little dust in his eyes, as our poet says of the bees, and all our ensigns and legions, with the great Pompey himself at the head of them, are routed and crushed to pieces; for it was he, as I take it, that Sertorious beat in Spain with those fine arms, which also served Eumenes against Antigonus, and Surena against Crassus:—

"Swarm to my bed like bees into their hives.

Declare for love, or war, she said; and frown'd:

No love I'll grant: to arms bid trumpets sound."

Hi motus animorum, atque hoc certamina tanta,

Pulveris exigui jactu compressa quiescent.

"Yet at thy will these dreadful conflicts cease,

Throw but a little dust and all is peace."

Let us but slip our flies after them, and they will have the force and courage to defeat them. Of fresh memory, the Portuguese having besieged the city of Tamly, in the territory of Xiatine, the inhabitants of the place brought a great many hives, of which are great plenty in that place, upon the wall; and with fire drove the bees so furiously upon the enemy that they gave over the enterprise, not being able to stand their attacks and endure their stings; and so the citizens, by this new sort of relief, gained liberty and the victory with so wonderful a fortune, that at the return of their defenders from the battle they found they had not lost so much as one. The souls of emperors and cobblers are cast in the same mould; the weight and importance of the actions of princes considered, we persuade ourselves that they must be produced by some as weighty and important causes; but we are deceived; for they are pushed on, and pulled back in their motions, by the same springs that we are in our little undertakings. The same reason that makes us wrangle with a neighbour causes a war betwixt princes; the same reason that makes us whip a lackey, falling into the hands of a king makes him ruin a whole province. They are as lightly moved as we, but they are able to do more. In a gnat and an elephant the passion is the same.

As to fidelity, there is no animal in the world so treacherous as man. Our histories have recorded the violent pursuits that dogs have made after the murderers of their masters. King Pyrrhus observing a dog that watched a dead man's body, and understanding that he had for three days together performed that office, commanded that the body should be buried, and took the dog along with him. One day, as he was at a general muster of his army, this dog, seeing his master's murderers, with great barking and extreme signs of anger flew upon them, and by this first accusation awakened the revenge of this murder, which was soon after perfected by form of justice. As much was done by the dog of the wise Hesiod, who convicted the sons of Ganictor of Naupactus of the murder committed on the person of his master. Another dog being to guard a temple at Athens, having spied a sacrilegious thief carrying away the finest jewels, fell to barking at him with all his force, but the warders not awaking at the noise, he followed him, and day being broke, kept off at a little distance, without losing sight of him; if he offered him any thing to eat he would not take it, but would wag his tail at all the passengers he met, and took whatever they gave him; and if the thief laid down to sleep, he likewise stayed upon the same place. The news of this dog being come to the warders of the temple they put themselves upon the pursuit, inquiring of the colour of the dog, and at last found him in the city of Cromyon, and the thief also, whom they brought back to Athens, where he got his reward; and the judges, in consideration of this good office, ordered a certain measure of corn for the dog's daily sustenance, at the public charge, and the priests to take care of it. Plutarch delivers this story for a certain truth, and that it happened in the age wherein he lived.

As to gratitude (for I think we need bring this word into a little repute), this one example, which Apion reports himself to have been an eye-witness of, shall suffice.

"One day," says he, "at Rome, they entertained the people with the sight of the fighting of several strange beasts, and principally of lions of an unusual size; there was one amongst the rest who, by his furious deportment, by the strength and largeness of his limbs, and by his loud and dreadful roaring, attracted the eyes of all the spectators. Amongst other slaves that were presented to the people in this combat of beasts there was one Androdus, of Dacia, belonging to a Roman lord of consular dignity. This lion having seen him at a distance first made a sudden stop, as it were in a wondering posture, and then softly approached nearer in a gentle and peaceable manner, as if it were to enter into acquaintance with him. This being done, and being now assured of what he sought for, he began to wag his tail, as dogs do when they flatter their masters, and to kiss and lick the hands and thighs of the poor wretch, who was beside himself, and almost dead with fear. Androdus being by this kindness of the lion a little come to himself, and having taken so much heart as to consider and know him, it was a singular pleasure to see the joy and caresses that passed betwixt them. At which the people breaking into loud acclamations of joy, the emperor caused the slave to be called, to know from him the cause of so strange an event; who thereupon told him a new and a very strange story: "My master," said he, "being pro-consul in Africa, I was constrained, by his severity and cruel usage, being daily beaten, to steal from him and run away; and, to hide myself secretly from a person of so great authority in the province, I thought it my best way to fly to the solitudes, sands, and uninhabitable parts of that country, resolving that in case the means of supporting life should chance to fail me, to make some shift or other to kill myself. The sun being excessively hot at noon, and the heat intolerable, I lit upon a private and almost inaccessible cave, and went into it Soon after there came in to me this lion, with one foot wounded and bloody, complaining and groaning with the pain he endured. At his coming I was exceeding afraid; but he having spied me hid in the comer of his den, came gently to me, holding out and showing me his wounded foot, as if he demanded my assistance in his distress. I then drew out a great splinter he had got there, and, growing a little more familiar with him, squeezing the wound thrust out the matter, dirt, and gravel which was got into it, and wiped and cleansed it the best I could. He, finding himself something better, and much eased of his pain, laid him down to rest, and presently fell asleep with his foot in my hand.

From that time forward he and I lived together in this cave three whole years upon one and the same diet; for of the beasts that he killed in hunting he always brought me the best pieces, which I roasted in the sun for want of fire, and so ate it. At last, growing weary of this wild and brutish life, the lion being one day gone abroad to hunt for our ordinary provision, I departed thence, and the third day after was taken by the soldiers, who brought me from Africa to this city to my master, who presently condemned me to die, and to be thus exposed to the wild beasts. Now, by what I see, this lion was also taken soon after, who has now sought to recompense me for the benefit and cure that he received at my hands." This is the story that Androdus told the emperor, which he also conveyed from hand to hand to the people; wherefore, at the general request, he was absolved from his sentence and set at liberty, and the lion was, by order of the people, presented to him. "We afterwards saw," says Apion, "Androdus leading this lion, in nothing but a small leash, from tavern to tavern at Rome, and receiving what money every body would give him, the lion being so gentle as to suffer himself to be covered with the flowers that the people threw upon him, every one that met him saying, 'There goes the lion that entertained the man; there goes the man that cured the lion.'"

We often lament the loss of beasts we love, and so do they the loss of us:—

>Post, bellator equus, positis insignibus, thon
>
>It lacrymans, guttisque humectt grandibus ora.

>"To close the pomp, thon, the steed of state.
>
>Is led, the fun'ral of his lord to wait.
>
>Stripped of his trappings, with a sullen pace
>
>He walks, and the big tears run rolling down his face."

As some nations have their wives in common, and some others have every one his own, is not the same seen among beasts, and marriages better kept than ours? As to the society and confederation they make amongst themselves, to league together and to give one another mutual assistance, is it not known that oxen, hogs, and other animals, at the cry of any of their kind that we offend, all the herd run to his aid and embody for his defence? The fish Scarus, when he has swallowed the angler's hook, his fellows all crowd about him and gnaw the line in pieces; and if, by chance, one be got into the bow net, the others present him their tails on the outside, which he holding fast with his teeth, they after that manner disengage and draw him out.

Mullets, when one of their companions is engaged, cross the line over their back, and, with a fin they have there, indented like a saw, cut and saw it asunder. As to the particular offices that we receive from one another for the service of life, there are several like examples amongst them. 'Tis said that the whale never moves that she has not always before her a little fish like the sea-gudgeon, for this reason called the guide-fish, whom the whale follows, suffering himself to be led and turned with as great facility as the rudder guides the ship; in recompense of which service also, whereas all the other things, whether beast or vessel, that enter into the dreadful gulf of this monster's mouth, are immediately lost and swallowed up, this little fish retires into it in great security, and there sleeps, during which time the whale never stirs; but so soon as ever it goes out he immediately follows it; and if by accident he loses the sight of his little guide, he goes wandering here and there, and strikes his sides against the rocks like a ship that has lost her helm; which Plutarch affirms to have seen in the island of Anticyra. There is a like society betwixt the little bird called the wren and the crocodile. The wren serves for a sentinel over this great animal; and if the ichneumon, his mortal enemy, approach to fight him, this little bird, for fear lest he should surprise him asleep, both with his voice and bill rouses him and gives him notice of his danger. He feeds of this monster's leavings, who receives him familiarly into his mouth, suffering him to peck in his jaws and betwixt his teeth, and thence to pick out the bits of flesh that remain; and when he has a mind to shut his mouth, he first gives the bird warning to go out by closing it by little and little, and without bruising or doing it any harm at all. The shell-fish called the naker, lives in the same intelligence with the shrimp, a little sort of animal of the lobster kind, which serves him in the nature of a porter, sitting at the opening of the shell, which the naker keeps always gaping and open till the shrimp sees some little fish, proper for their prey, within the hollow of the shell, where she enters too, and pinches the naker so to the quick that she is forced to close her shell, where they two together devour the prey they have trapped in their fort. In the manner of living of the tunnies we observe a singular knowledge of the three parts of mathematics. As to astrology, they teach it men, for they stay in the place where they are surprised by the brumal solstice, and never stir thence till the next equinox; for which reason Aristotle himself attributes to them this science. As to geometry and arithmetic, they always form their numbers in the figure of a cube, every way square, and make up the body of a battalion, solid, close, and environed round with six equal sides, and swim in this square order, as large behind as before; so that whoever in seeing them can count one rank may easily number the whole troop, by reason that the depth is equal to the breadth, and the breadth to the length.

As to magnanimity, it will be hard to exhibit a better instance of it than in the example of the great dog sent to Alexander the Great from the Indies. They first brought him a stag to encounter, next a boar, and after that a bear, all which he slighted, and disdained to stir from his place; but when he saw a lion he then immediately roused himself, evidently manifesting that he declared that alone worthy to enter the lists with him. Touching repentance and the acknowledgment of faults, 'tis reported of an elephant that, having in the impetuosity of his rage killed his keeper, he fell into so extreme a sorrow that he would never after eat, but starved himself to death. And as to clemency, 'tis said of a tiger, the most cruel of all beasts, that a kid having been put in to him, he suffered a two days' hunger rather than hurt it, and the third broke the grate he was shut up in, to seek elsewhere for prey; so unwilling he was to fall upon the kid, his familiar and his guest, And as to the laws of familiarity and agreement, formed by conversation, it ordinarily happens that we bring up cats, dogs, and hares, tame together.

But that which seamen by experience know, and particularly in the Sicilian Sea, of the quality of the halcyons, surpasses all human thought of what kind of animal has nature even so much honoured the birth? The poets indeed say that one only island, Delos, which was before a floating island, was fixed for the service of Latona's lying-in; but God has ordered that the whole ocean should be stayed, made stable and smooth, without waves, without winds or rain, whilst the halcyon produces her young, which is just about the solstice, the shortest day of the year; so that by her privilege we have seven days and seven nights in the very heart of winter wherein we may sail without danger. Their females never have to do with any other male but their own, whom they serve and assist all their lives, without ever forsaking him. If he becomes weak and broken with age, they take him upon their shoulders and carry him from place to place, and serve him till death. But the most inquisitive into the secrets of nature could never yet arrive at the knowledge of the wonderful fabric wherewith the halcyon builds her nest for her little ones, nor guess at the materials. Plutarch, who has seen and handled many of them, thinks it is the bones of some fish which she joins and binds together, interlacing them, some lengthwise and others across, and adding ribs and hoops in such manner that she forms at last a round vessel fit to launch; which being done, and the building finished, she carries it to the beach, where the sea beating gently against it shows where she is to mend what is not well jointed and knit, and where better to fortify the seams that are leaky, that open at the beating of the waves; and, on the contrary, what is well built and has had the due finishing, the beating of the waves does so close and bind together that it is not to be broken or cracked by blows either of stone or iron without very much ado. And that which is more to be admired is the proportion and figure of the cavity within, which is composed and proportioned after such a manner as not to receive or admit any other thing than the bird that built it; for to any thing else it is so impenetrable, close, and shut, nothing can enter, not so much as the water of the sea. This is a very dear description of this building, and borrowed from a very good hand; and yet me-thinks it does not give us sufficient light into the difficulty of this architecture. Now from what vanity can it proceed to despise and look down upon, and disdainfully to interpret, effects that we can neither imitate nor comprehend?

To pursue a little further this equality and correspondence betwixt us and beasts, the privilege our soul so much glorifies herself upon, of things she conceives to her own law, of striping all things that come to her of their mortal and corporeal qualities, of ordering and placing things she conceives worthy her taking notice of, stripping and divesting them of their corruptible qualities, and making them to lay aside length, breadth, depth, weight, colour, smell, roughness, smoothness, hardness, softness, and all sensible accidents, as mean and superfluous vestments, to accommodate them to her own immortal and spiritual condition; as Rome and Paris, for example, that I have in my fancy, Paris that I imagine, I imagine and comprehend it without greatness and without place, without stone, without plaster, and without wood; this very same privilege, I say, seems evidently to be in beasts; for a courser accustomed to trumpets, to musket-shots, and battles, whom we see start and tremble in his sleep and stretched upon his litter, as if he were in a fight; it is almost certain that he conceives in his soul the beat of a drum without noise, and an army without arms and without body:—

Quippe videbis equos fortes, cum membra jacebunt

In somnis, sudare tamen, spirareque spe,

Et quasi de palm summas contendere vires:

"You shall see maneg'd horses in their sleep

Sweat, snort, start, tremble, and a clutter keep,

As if with all their force they striving were

The victor's palm proudly away to bear:"

the hare, that a greyhound imagines in his sleep, after which we see him pant so whilst he sleeps, stretch out his tail, shake his legs, and perfectly represents all the motions of a course, is a hare without fur and without bones:—

Venantumque canes in molli spe quiete

Jactant crura tamen subito, vocesque repente

Mittunt, et crebras reducunt naribus auras,

Ut vestigia si teneant inventa ferarum:

Expergeftique sequuntur inania spe

Cervorum simulacra, fag quasi dedita cernant;

Donee discussis redeant erroribus ad se:

"And hounds stir often in their quiet rest,

Spending their mouths, as if upon a quest,

Snuff, and breathe quick and short, as if they went

In a full chase upon a burning scent:

Nay, being wak'd, imagin'd stags pursue,

> As if they had them in their real view,
>
> Till, having shook themselves more broad awake,
>
> They do at last discover the mistake:"

the watch-dogs, that we often observe to snarl in their dreams, and afterwards bark out, and start up as if they perceived some stranger at hand; the stranger that their soul discerns is a man spiritual and imperceptible, without dimension, without colour, and without being:—

> Consueta domi catulorum blanda propago
>
> Degere, spe levem ex oculis volucremque soporem
>
> Discutere, et corpus de terra corripere instant,
>
> Proinde quasi ignotas facies atque ora tuantur.

> "The fawning whelps of household curs will rise,
>
> And, shaking the soft slumber from their eyes,
>
> Oft bark and stare at ev'ry one within,
>
> As upon faces they had never seen."

to the beauty of the body, before I proceed any further I should know whether or no we are agreed about the description. 'Tis likely we do not well know what beauty is in nature and in general, since to our own human beauty we give so many divers forms, of which, were there any natural rule and prescription, we should know it in common, as the heat of the fire. But we fancy the forms according to our own appetite and liking:—

Turpis Romano Belgicus ore color:

"A German hue ill suits, a Roman face."

The Indians paint it black and tawny, with great swelled lips, wide flat noses and load the cartilage betwixt the nostrils with great rings of gold, to make it hang down to the mouth; as also the under lip with great hoops, enriched with precious stones, that weigh them down to fall upon the chin, it being with them a singular grace to show their teeth, even below the roots. In Peru the greatest ears are the most beautiful, which they stretch out as far as they can by art. And a man now living says that he has seen in an eastern nation this care of enlarging them in so great repute, and the ear loaded with so ponderous jewels, that he did with great ease put his arm, sleeve and all, through the hole of an ear. There are elsewhere nations that take great care to black their teeth, and hate to see them white, whilst others paint them red. The women are reputed more beautiful, not only in Biscay, but elsewhere, for having their heads shaved; and, which is more, in certain frozen countries, as Pliny reports. The Mexicans esteem a low forehead a great beauty, and though they shave all other parts, they nourish hair on the forehead and increase it by art, and have great breasts in so great reputation that they affect to give their children suck over their shoulders. We should paint deformity so. The Italians fashion it gross and massy; the Spaniards gaunt and slender; and amongst us one has it white, another brown; one soft and delicate, another strong and vigorous; one will have his mistress soft and gentle, others haughty and majestic. Just as the preference in beauty that Plato attributes to the spherical figure the Epicureans gave rather to the pyramidal or square, and cannot swallow a god in the form of a bowl. But, be it how it will, nature has no more privileged us in this from her common laws than in the rest And if we will judge ourselves aright, we shall find that, if there be some animals less favoured in this than we, there are others, and in greater number, that are more; a multis animalibus decore vincimur "Many animals surpass us in beauty," even among the terrestrial, our compatriots; for as to those of sea, setting the figure aside, which cannot fall into any manner of proportion, being so much another thing in colour, clearness, smoothness, and arrangement, we sufficiently give place to them; and no less, in all qualities, to the aerial. And this prerogative that the poets make such a mighty matter of, our erect stature, looking towards heaven our original,

    Pronaque cum spectent animalia ctera terrain,

    Os homini sublime ddit, columque tueri

    Jussit, et erectos ad sidera tollere vultus,

    "Whilst all the brutal creatures downward bend

    Their sight, and to their earthly mother tend,

    He set man's face aloft, that, with his eyes

    Uplifted, he might view the starry skies,"

is truly poetical; for there are several little beasts who have their sight absolutely turned towards heaven; and I find the gesture of camels and ostriches much higher raised and more erect than ours. What animals have not their faces above and not before, and do not look opposite, as we do; and that do not in their natural posture discover as much of heaven and earth as man? And what qualities of our bodily constitution, in Plato and Cicero, may not indifferently serve a thousand sorts of beasts? Those that most resemble us are the most despicable and deformed of all the herd; for those, as to outward appearance and form of visage, are baboons:—

Simia quam similis, turpissima bestia, nobis?

"How like to man, in visage and in shape,

Is, of all beasts the most uncouth, the ape?"

as to the internal and vital parts, the hog. In earnest, when I consider man stark naked, even in that sex which seems to have greatest share of beauty, his defects, natural subjection, and imperfections, I find that we have more reason than any other animal, to cover ourselves; and are to be excused from borrowing of those to whom nature has in this been kinder than to us, to trick ourselves out with their beauties, and hide ourselves under their spoils, their wool, feathers, hair, and silk. Let us observe, as to the rest, that man is the sole animal whose nudities offend his own companions, and the only one who in his natural actions withdraws and hides himself from his own kind. And really 'tis also an effect worth consideration, that they who are masters in the trade prescribe, as a remedy for amorous passions, the full and free view of the body a man desires; for that to cool the ardour there needs no more but freely and fully to see what he loves:—

Ille quod obscnas in aperto corpore partes

Viderat, in cursu qui fuit, hsit amor.

"The love that's tilting when those parts appear

Open to view, flags in the hot career,"

And, although this receipt may peradventure proceed from a nice and cold humour, it is notwithstanding a very great sign of our deficiencies that use and acquaintance should make us disgust one another. It is not modesty, so much as cunning and prudence, that makes our ladies so circumspect to refuse us admittance into their cabinets before they are painted and tricked up for the public view:—

Nec Veneres nostras hoc fallit; quo magis ips

Omnia summopere hos vit postscenia celant,

Quos retinere volunt, adstrictoque esse in amore:

"Of this our ladies are full well aware,

Which make them, with such privacy and care,

Behind the scene all those defects remove,

Likely to check the flame of those they love,"

whereas, in several animals there is nothing that we do not love, and that does not please our senses; so that from their very excrements we do not only extract wherewith to heighten our sauces, but also our richest ornaments and perfumes. This discourse reflects upon none but the ordinary sort of women, and is not so sacrilegious as to comprehend those divine, supernatural, and extraordinary beauties, which we see shine occasionally among us like stars under a corporeal and terrestrial veil.

As to the rest, the very share that we allow to beasts of the bounty of nature, by our own confession, is very much to their advantage. We attribute to ourselves imaginary and fantastic good, future and absent good, for which human capacity cannot of herself be responsible; or good, that we falsely attribute to ourselves by the license of opinion, as reason, knowledge, and honour, and leave to them for their dividend, essential, durable, and palpable good, as peace, repose, security, innocence, and health; health, I say, the fairest and richest present that nature can make us. Insomuch that philosophy, even the Stoic, is so bold as to say, "That Heraclitus and Pherecides, could they have trucked their wisdom for health, and have delivered themselves, the one of his dropsy, and the other of the lousy disease that tormented him, they had done well." By which they set a greater value upon wisdom, comparing and putting it into the balance with health, than they do with this other proposition, which is also theirs; they say that if Circe had presented Ulysses with the two potions, the one to make a fool become a wise man, and the other to make a wise man become a fool, that Ulysses ought rather to have chosen the last, than consent to that by which Circe changed his human figure into that of a beast; and say that wisdom itself would have spoke to him after this manner: "Forsake me, let me alone, rather than lodge me under the body and figure of an ass." How! the philosophers, then will abandon this great and divine wisdom for this corporeal and terrestrial covering? It is then no more by reason, by discourse, and by the soul, that we excel beasts; 'tis by our beauty, our fair complexion, and our fine symmetry of parts, for which we must quit our intelligence, our prudence, and all the rest. Well, I accept this open and free confession; certainly they knew that those parts, upon which we so much value ourselves, are no other than vain fancy. If beasts then had all the virtue, knowledge, wisdom, and stoical perfection, they would still be beasts, and would not be comparable to man, miserable, wicked, mad, man. For, in short, whatever is not as we are is nothing worth; and God, to procure himself an esteem among us, must put himself into that shape, as we shall show anon. By which it appears that it is not upon any true ground of reason, but by a foolish pride and vain opinion, that we prefer ourselves before other animals, and separate ourselves from their society and condition.

But to return to what I was upon before; we have for our part inconstancy, irresolution, incertitude, sorrow, superstition, solicitude of things to come, even after we shall be no more, ambition, avarice, jealousy, envy, irregular, frantic, and untamed appetites, war, lying, disloyalty, detraction, and curiosity. Doubtless, we have strangely overpaid this fine reason, upon which we so much glorify ourselves, and this capacity of judging and knowing, if we have bought it at the price of this infinite number of passions to which we are eternally subject. Unless we shall also think fit, as even Socrates does, to add to the counterpoise that notable prerogative above beasts, That whereas nature has prescribed them certain seasons and limits for the delights of Venus, she has given us the reins at all hours and all seasons." Ut vinum ogrotis, quia prodest rar, nocet sopissime, melius est non adhibere omnino, quam, spe dubio salutis, in apertam per-niciem incurrere; sic, haud scio an melius fuerit humano generi motum istum celerem cogitationis, acumen, solertiam, quam rationem vocamus, quoniam pestifera sint multis, ad-modum paucis saluiaria, non dari omnino, quam tam muniice et tam large dari? As it falls out that wine often hurting the sick, and very rarely doing them good, it is better not to give them any at all than to run into an apparent danger out of hope of an uncertain benefit, so I know not whether it had not been better for mankind that this quick motion, this penetration, this subtlety that we call reason, had not been given to man at all; considering how pestiferous it is to many, and useful but to few, than to have been conferred in so abundant manner, and with so liberal a hand." Of what advantage can we conceive the knowledge of so many things was to Yarro and Aristotle? Did it exempt them from human inconveniences? Were they by it freed from the accidents that lay heavy upon the shoulders of a porter? Did they extract from their logic any consolation for the gout? Or, for knowing how this humour is lodged in the joints, did they feel it the less? Did they enter into composition with death by knowing that some nations rejoice at his approach; or with cuckoldry, by knowing that in some parts of the world wives are in common? On the contrary, having been reputed the greatest men for knowledge, the one amongst the Romans and the other amongst the Greeks, and in a time when learning did most flourish, we have not heard, nevertheless, that they had any particular excellence in their lives; nay, the Greek had enough to do to clear himself from some notable blemishes in his. Have we observed that pleasure and health have a better relish with him that understands astrology and grammar than with others?

    Illiterati num minus nervi rigent?

"Th' illiterate ploughman is as fit

For Venus' service as the wit:"

or shame and poverty less troublesome to the first than to the last?

>Scilicet et morbis et debilitate carebis,
>
>Et luctum et curam effugies, et tempora vit
>
>Longa tibi post hc fato meliore dabuntur.

>"Disease thy couch shall flee,
>
>And sorrow and care; yes, thou, be sure, wilt see
>
>Long years of happiness, till now unknown."

I have known in my time a hundred artisans, a hundred labourers, wiser and more happy than the rectors of the university, and whom I had much rather have resembled. Learning, methinks, has its place amongst the necessary, things of life, as glory, nobility, dignity, or at the most, as beauty, riches, and such other qualities, which indeed are useful to it, but remotely, and more by opinion than by nature. We stand very little more in need of offices, rules, and laws of living in our society, than cranes and ants do in theirs; and yet we see that these carry themselves very regularly without erudition. If man was wise, he would take the true value of every thing according as it was useful and proper to his life. Whoever will number us by our actions and deportments will find many more excellent men amongst the ignorant than among the learned; aye, in all sorts of virtue. Old Rome seems to me to have been of much greater value, both for peace and war, than that learned Rome that ruined itself. And, though all the rest should be equal, yet integrity and innocency would remain to the ancients, for they cohabit singularly well with simplicity. But I will leave this discourse, that would lead me farther than I am willing to follow; and shall only say this further, 'tis only humility and submission that can make a complete good man. We are not to leave the knowledge of his duty to every man's own judgment; we are to prescribe it to him, and not suffer him to choose it at his own discretion; otherwise, according to the imbecility, and infinite variety of our reasons and opinions, we should at large forge ourselves duties that would, as Epicurus says, enjoin us to eat one another.

The first law that ever God gave to man was a law of pure obedience; it was a commandment naked and simple, wherein man had nothing to inquire after, nor to dispute; forasmuch as to obey is the proper office of a rational soul, acknowledging a heavenly superior and benefactor. From obedience and submission spring all other virtues, as all sin does from selfopinion. And, on the contrary, the first temptation that by the devil was offered to human nature, its first poison insinuated itself into us by the promise made us of knowledge and wisdom; Eritis sicut Dii, scientes bonum et malum. "Ye shall be as gods, knowing good and evil." And the sirens, in Homer, to allure Ulysses, and draw him within the danger of their snares, offered to give him knowledge. The plague of man is the opinion of wisdom; and for this reason it is that ignorance is so recommended to us, by our religion, as proper to faith and obedience; Cavete ne quis vos decipiat per philosophiam et inanes seductiones, secundum elementa mundi. "Take heed, lest any man deceive you by philosophy and vain deceit, after the tradition of men, and the rudiments of the world." There is in this a general consent amongst all sorts of philosophers, that the sovereign good consists in the tranquillity of the soul and body; but where shall we find it?

    Ad summum, sapiens uno minor est Jove, dives,

Liber, honoratus, pulcher, rex deniqne regum;

Prcipue sanus, nisi cum pituita molesta est:

"In short, the wise is only less than Jove,

Rich, free, and handsome; nay, a king above

All earthly kings; with health supremely blest,

Excepting when a cold disturbs his rest!"

It seems, in truth, that nature, for the consolation of our miserable and wretched state, has only given us presumption for our inheritance. 'Tis as Epictetus says, that man has nothing properly his own, but the use of his opinion; we have nothing but wind and smoke for our portion. The gods have health in essence, says philosophy, and sickness in intelligence. Man, on the contrary, possesses his goods by fancy, his ills in essence. We have reason to magnify the power of our imagination; for all our goods are only in dream. Hear this poor calamitous animal huff! "There is nothing," says Cicero, "so charming as the employment of letters; of letters, I say, by means whereof the infinity of things, the immense grandeur of nature, the heavens even in this world, the earth, and the seas are discovered to us; 'tis they that have taught us religion, moderation, and the grandeur of courage, and that have rescued our souls from darkness, to make her see all things, high, low, first, last, and middling; 'tis they that furnish us wherewith to live happily and well, and conduct us to pass over our lives without displeasure, and without offence." Does not this man seem to speak of the condition of the ever-living and almighty God? But as to effects, a thousand little countrywomen have lived lives more equal, more sweet, and constant than his.

    Deus ille fuit, deus, inclyte Memmi,

Qui princeps vit rationem invenit earn, qu

Nunc appellatur sapientia; quique per artem

Fluctibus tantis vitam, tantisque tenebris,

In tam tranquilla et tam clara luce locavit:

"That god, great Memmus, was a god no doubt

Who, prince of life, first found that reason out

Now wisdom called; and by his art, who did

That life in tempests tost, and darkness hid,

Place in so great a calm, and clear a light:"

here are brave ranting words; but a very slight accident put this man's understanding in a worse condition than that of the meanest shepherd, notwithstanding this instructing god, this divine wisdom. Of the same stamp and impudence is the promise of Democritus's book: "I am going to speak of all things;" and that foolish title that Aristotle prefixes to one of his, order only afforded him a few lucid intervals which he employed in composing his book, and at last made him kill himself,—Eusebius's Chronicon.

Of the Mortal Gods; and the judgment of Chrysippus, that "Dion was as virtuous as God;" and my Seneca himself says, that "God had given him life; but that to live well was his own;" conformably to this other: In virtute vere gloriamur; quod non contingeret, si id donum Deo, non nobis haberemus: "We truly glory in our virtue; which would not be, if it was given us of God, and not by ourselves;" this is also Seneca's saying; "that the wise man hath fortitude equal with God, but that his is in spite of human frailty, wherein therefore he more than equals God." There is nothing so ordinary as to meet with sallies of the like temerity; there is none of us, who take so much offence to see himself equalled with God, as he does to see himself undervalued by being ranked with other creatures; so much more are we jealous of our own interest than that of our Creator.

But we must trample under foot this foolish vanity, and briskly and boldly shake the ridiculous foundation upon which these false opinions are founded. So long as man shall believe he has any means and power of himself, he will never acknowledge what he owes to his Maker; his eggs shall always be chickens, as the saying is; we must therefore strip him to his shirt. Let us see some notable examples of the effects of his philosophy: Posidonius being tormented with a disease so painful as made him writhe his arms and gnash his teeth, thought he sufficiently scorned the dolour, by crying out against it: "Thou mayst do thy worst, I will not confess that thou art an evil." He was as sensible of the pain as my footman, but he made a bravado of bridling his tongue, at least, and restraining it within the laws of his sect: Re succumbere non oportebat, verbis gloriantem. "It did not become him, that spoke so big, to confess his frailty when he came to the test." Arcesilas being ill of the gout, and Car-neades, who had come to see him, going away troubled at his condition, he called him back, and showing him his feet and breast: "There is nothing comes thence hither," said he. This has something a better grace, for he feels himself in pain, and would be disengaged from it; but his heart, notwithstanding, is not conquered nor subdued by it. The other stands more obstinately to his point, but, I fear, rather verbally than really. And Dionysius Heracleotes, afflicted with a vehement smarting in his eyes, was reduced to quit these stoical resolutions. But even though knowledge should, in effect, do as they say, and could blunt the point, and dull the edge, of the misfortunes that attend us, what does she, more than what ignorance does more purely and evidently?—The philosopher Pyrrho, being at sea in very great danger, by reason of a mighty storm, presented nothing to the imitation of those who were with him, in that extremity, but a hog they had on board, that was fearless and unconcerned at the tempest. Philosophy, when she has said all she can, refers us at last to the example of a gladiator, wrestler, or muleteer, in which sort of people we commonly observe much less apprehension of death, sense of pain, and other inconveniences, and more of endurance, than ever knowledge furnished any one withal, that was not born and bred to hardship. What is the cause that we make incisions, and cut the tender limbs of an infant, and those of a horse, more easily than our own—but ignorance only? How many has mere force of imagination made sick? We often see men cause themselves to be let blood, purged, and physicked, to be cured of diseases they only feel in opinion.—When real infirmities fail us, knowledge lends us her's; that colour, that complexion, portend some catarrhous defluxion; this hot season threatens us with a fever; this breach in the life-line of your left hand gives you notice of some near and dangerous indisposition; and at last she roundly attacks health itself; saying, this sprightliness and vigour of youth cannot continue in this posture; there must be blood taken, and the heat abated, lest it turn against yourself. Compare the life of a man subjected to such imaginations, to that of a labourer that suffers himself to be led by his natural appetite, measuring things only by the present sense, without knowledge, and without prognostic, that feels no pain or sickness, but when he is really ill. Whereas the other has the stone in his soul, before he has it in his bladder; as if it were not time enough to suffer the evil when it shall come, he must anticipate it by fancy, and run to meet it.

What I say of physic may generally serve in example for all other sciences. Thence is derived that ancient opinion of the philosophers that placed the sovereign good in the discovery of the weakness of our judgment My ignorance affords me as much occasion of hope as of fear; and having no other rule for my health than that of the examples of others, and of events I see elsewhere upon the like occasion, I find of all sorts, and rely upon those which by comparison are most favourable to me. I receive health with open arms, free, full, and entire, and by so much the more whet my appetite to enjoy it, by how much it is at present less ordinary and more rare; so far am I from troubling its repose and sweetness with the bitterness of a new and constrained manner of living. Beasts sufficiently show us how much the agitation of our minds brings infirmities and diseases upon us. That which is told us of those of Brazil, that they never die but of old age, is attributed to the serenity and tranquillity of the air they live in; but I rather attribute it to the serenity and tranquillity of their souls, free from all passion, thought, or employment, extended or unpleasing, a people that pass over their lives in a wonderful simplicity and ignorance, without letters, without law, without king, or any manner of religion. And whence comes that, which we find by experience, that the heaviest and dullest men are most able; and the most to be desired in amorous performances; and that the love of a muleteer often renders itself more acceptable than that of a gentleman, if it be not that the agitation of the soul in the latter disturbs his physical ability, dissolves and tires it, as it also ordinarily troubles and tires itself. What puts the soul beside itself, and more usually throws it into madness, but her own promptness, vigour, and agility, and, finally, her own proper force? Of what is the most subtle folly made, but of the most subtle wisdom? As great friendships spring from great enmities, and vigorous health from mortal diseases, so from the rare and vivid agitations of our souls proceed the most wonderful and most distracted frenzies; 'tis but half a turn of the toe from the one to the other. In the actions of madmen we see how infinitely madness resembles the most vigorous operations of the soul. Who does not know how indiscernible the difference is betwixt folly and the sprightly elevations of a free soul, and the effects of a supreme and extraordinary virtue? Plato says that melancholy persons are the most capable of discipline, and the most excellent; and accordingly in none is there so great a propension to madness. Great wits are ruined by their own proper force and pliability; into what a condition, through his own agitation and promptness of fancy, is one of the most judicious, ingenious, and nearest formed, of any other Italian poet, to the air of the ancient and true poesy, lately fallen! Has he not vast obligation to this vivacity that has destroyed him? to this light that has blinded him? to this exact and subtle apprehension of reason that has put him beside his own? to this curious and laborious search after sciences, that has reduced him to imbecility? and to this rare aptitude to the exercises of the soul, that has rendered him without exercise and without soul? I was more angry, if possible, than compassionate, to see him at Ferrara in so pitiful a condition surviving himself, forgetting both himself and his works, which, without his knowledge, though before his face, have been published unformed and incorrect.

Would you have a man healthy, would you have him regular, and in a steady and secure posture? Muffle him up in the shades of stupidity and sloth. We must be made beasts to be made wise, and hoodwinked before we are fit to be led. And if one shall tell me that the advantage of having a cold and dull sense of pain and other evils, brings this disadvantage along with it, to render us consequently less sensible also in the fruition of good and pleasure, this is true; but the misery of our condition is such that we have not so much to enjoy as to avoid, and that the extremest pleasure does not affect us to the degree that a light grief does: Segnius homines bona quam mala sentiunt. We are not so sensible of the most perfect health as we are of the least sickness.

    Pungit

In cute vix sum ma violatum plagula corpus;

Quando valere nihil quemquam movet. Hoc juvat unum,

Quod me non torquet latus, aut pes;

Ctera quisquam Vix queat aut sanum sese, aut sentire valentem.

"The body with a little sting is griev'd,

When the most perfect health is not perceiv'd,

This only pleases me, that spleen nor gout

Neither offend my side nor wring my foot;

Excepting these, scarce any one can tell,

Or e'er observes, when he's in health and well."

Our well-being is nothing but the not being ill. Which is the reason why that sect of philosophers, which sets the greatest value upon pleasure, has yet fixed it chiefly in unconsciousness of pain. To be freed from ill is the greatest good that man can hope for or desire; as Ennius says,—

Nimium boni est, cui nihil est mali;

for that every tickling and sting which are in certain pleasures, and that seem to raise us above simple health and passiveness, that active, moving, and, I know not how, itching, and biting pleasure; even that very pleasure itself aims at nothing but insensibility as its mark. The appetite that carries us headlong to women's embraces has no other end but only to cure the torment of our ardent and furious desires, and only requires to be glutted and laid at rest, and delivered from the fever. And so of the rest. I say, then, that if simplicity conducts us to a state free from evil, she leads us to a very happy one according to our condition. And yet we are not to imagine it so stupid an insensibility as to be totally without sense; for Crantor had very good reason to controvert the insensibility of Epicurus, if founded so deep that the very first attack and birth of evils were not to be perceived: "I do not approve such an insensibility as is neither possible nor to be desired. I am very well content not to be sick; but if I am, I would know that I am so; and if a caustic be applied, or incisions made in any part, I would feel them." In truth, whoever would take away the knowledge and sense of evil, would at the same time eradicate the sense of pleasure, and finally annihilate man himself: Istud nihil dolere, non sine magn mercede contingit, immanitatis in animo, stuporis in corpore. "An insensibility that is not to be purchased but at the price of inhumanity in the soul, and of stupidity of the body." Evil appertains to man of course. Neither is pain always to be avoided, nor pleasure always pursued.

'Tis a great advantage to the honour of ignorance that knowledge itself throws us into its arms, when she finds herself puzzled to fortify us against the weight of evil; she is constrained to come to this composition, to give us the reins, and permit us to fly into the lap of the other, and to shelter ourselves under her protection from the strokes and injuries of fortune. For what else is her meaning when she instructs us to divert our thoughts from the ills that press upon us, and entertain them with the meditation of pleasures past and gone; to comfort ourselves in present afflictions with the remembrance of fled delights, and to call to our succour a vanished satisfaction, to oppose it to the discomfort that lies heavy upon us? Levationes gritudinum in avocatione a cogitand molesti, et revocation ad contemplandas voluptates, ponit; "He directs us to alleviate our grief and pains by rejecting unpleasant thoughts, and recalling agreeable ideas;" if it be not that where her power fails she would supply it with policy, and make use of sleight of hand where force of limbs will not serve her turn? For not only to a philosopher, but to any man in his right wits, when he has upon him the thirst of a burning fever, what satisfaction can it be to him to remember the pleasure he took in drinking Greek wine a month ago? It would rather only make matters worse to him:—

Che ricordarsi il ben doppia la noia.

"The thinking of pleasure doubles trouble."

Of the same stamp is this other counsel that philosophy gives, only to remember the happiness that is past, and to forget the misadventures we have undergone; as if we had the science of oblivion in our own power, and counsel, wherein we are yet no more to seek.

Suavis laborum est prteritorum rmoria.

"Sweet is the memory of by-gone pain."

How does philosophy, that should arm me to contend with fortune, and steel my courage to trample all human adversities under foot, arrive to this degree of cowardice to make me hide my head at this rate, and save myself by these pitiful and ridiculous shifts? For the memory represents to us not what we choose, but what she pleases; nay, there is nothing that so much imprints any thing in our memory as a desire to forget it. And 'tis a good way to retain and keep any thing safe in the soul to solicit her to lose it. And this is false: Est situm in nobis, ut et adversa quasi perpetua oblivione obruamus, et secunda jucunde et suaviter meminerimus; "it is in our power to bury, as it were, in a perpetual oblivion, all adverse accidents, and to retain a pleasant and delightful memory of our successes;" and this is true: Memini etiam quo nolo; oblivisci non possum quo volo. "I do also remember what I would not; but I cannot forget what I would." And whose counsel is this? His, qui se unies sapiervtem profiteri sit ausus; "who alone durst profess himself a wise man."

> Qui genus humanum ingenio superavit, et omnes
>
> Prstinxit stellas, exortus uti thereus Sol.

> "Who from mankind the prize of knowledge won,
>
> And put the stars out like the rising sun."

To empty and disfurnish the memory, is not this the true way to ignorance?

> Iners malorum remedium ignorantia est.

> "Ignorance is but a dull remedy for evils."

We find several other like precepts, whereby we are permitted to borrow frivolous appearances from the vulgar, where we find the strongest reason will not answer the purpose, provided they administer satisfaction and comfort Where they cannot cure the wound, they are content to palliate and benumb it I believe they will not deny this, that if they could add order and constancy in a state of life that could maintain itself in ease and pleasure by some debility of judgment, they would accept it:—

> Potare, et spargere flores
>
> Incipiam, patiarque vel inconsultus haberi.

> "Give me to drink, and, crown'd with flowers, despise
>
> The grave disgrace of being thought unwise."

There would be a great many philosophers of Lycas's mind this man, being otherwise of very regular manners, living quietly and contentedly in his family, and not failing in any office of his duty, either towards his own or strangers, and very carefully preserving himself from hurtful things, became, nevertheless, by some distemper in his brain, possessed with a conceit that he was perpetually in the theatre, a spectator of the finest sights and the best comedies in the world; and being cured by the physicians of his frenzy, was hardly prevented from endeavouring by suit to compel them to restore him again to his pleasing imagination:—

> Pol! me occidistis, amici,
>
> Non servastis, ait; cui sic extorta voluptas,
>
> Et demptus per vim mentis gratissimus error;

> "By heaven! you've killed me, friends, outright,
>
> And not preserved me; since my dear delight
>
> And pleasing error, by my better sense
>
> Unhappily return'd, is banished hence;"

with a madness like that of Thrasylaus the son of Pythodorus, who made himself believe that all the ships that weighed anchor from the port of Pirus, and that came into the haven, only made their voyages for his profit; congratulating them upon their successful navigation, and receiving them with the greatest joy; and when his brother Crito caused him to be restored to his better understanding, he infinitely regretted that sort of condition wherein he had lived with so much delight and free from all anxiety of mind. 'Tis according to the old Greek verse, that "there is a great deal of convenience in not being over-wise."

And Ecclesiastes, "In much wisdom there is much sorrow;" and "Who gets wisdom gets labour and trouble."

Even that to which philosophy consents in general, that last remedy which she applies to all sorts of necessities, to put an end to the life we are not able to endure. Placet?—Pare. Non placet?—Qucumque vis, exi. Pungit dolor?—Vel fodiat sane. Si nudus es, da jugulum; sin tectus armis Vulcaniis, id est fortitudine, rsist; "Does it please?—Obey it. Not please?—Go where thou wilt. Does grief prick thee,—nay, stab thee?—If thou art naked, present thy throat; if covered with the arms of Vulcan, that is, fortitude, resist it." And this word, so used in the Greek festivals, aut bibat, aut abeat, "either drink or go," which sounds better upon the tongue of a Gascon, who naturally changes the h into v, than on that of Cicero:—

> Vivere si recte nescis, decede peritis.
>
> Lusisti satis, edisti satis, atque bibisti;
>
> Tempus abire tibi est, ne potum largius quo
>
> Rideat et pulset lasciva decentius tas.

> "If to live well and right thou dost not know,

Give way, and leave thy place to those that do.

Thou'st eaten, drunk, and play'd to thy content,

'Tis time to make thy parting compliment,

Lest youth, more decent in their follies, scoff

The nauseous scene, and hiss thee reeling off;"

What is it other than a confession of his impotency, and a sending back not only to ignorance, to be there in safety, but even to stupidity, insensibility, and nonentity?

Democritum postquam matura vetustas

Admonuit memorem motus languescere mentis;

Sponte sua letho caput obvius obtulit ipse.

"Soon as, through age, Democritus did find

A manifest decadence in his mind,

He thought he now surviv'd to his own wrong,

And went to meet his death, that stay'd too long."

'Tis what Antisthenes said, "That a man should either make provision of sense to understand, or of a halter to hang himself;" and what Chrysippus alleged upon this saying of the poet Tyrtus:—

"Or to arrive at virtue or at death;"

and Crates said, "That love would be cured by hunger, if not by time; and whoever disliked these two remedies, by a rope." That Sextius, of whom both Seneca and Plutarch speak with so high an encomium, having applied himself, all other things set aside, to the study of philosophy, resolved to throw himself into the sea, seeing the progress of his studies too tedious and slow. He ran to find death, since he could not overtake knowledge. These are the words of the law upon the subject: "If peradventure some great inconvenience happen, for which there is no remedy, the haven is near, and a man may save himself by swimming out of his body as out of a leaky skiff; for 'tis the fear of dying, and not the love of life, that ties the fool to his body."

As life renders itself by simplicity more pleasant, so more innocent and better, also it renders it as I was saying before: "The simple and ignorant," says St. Paul, "raise themselves up to heaven and take possession of it; and we, with all our knowledge, plunge ourselves into the infernal abyss." I am neither swayed by Valentinian, a professed enemy to all learning and letters, nor by Licinius, both Roman emperors, who called them the poison and pest of all political government; nor by Mahomet, who, as 'tis said, interdicted all manner of learning to his followers; but the example of the great Lycurgus, and his authority, with the reverence of the divine Lacedemonian policy, so great, so admirable, and so long flourishing in virtue and happiness, without any institution or practice of letters, ought certainly to be of very great weight. Such as return from the new world discovered by the Spaniards in our fathers' days, testify to us how much more honestly and regularly those nations live, without magistrate and without law, than ours do, where there are more officers and lawyers than there are of other sorts of men and business:—

  Di cittatorie piene, e di libelli,

D'esamine, e di carte di procure,

Hanno le mani e il seno, e gran fastelli

Di chioge, di consigli, et di letture:

Per cui le faculta de* poverelli

Non sono mai nelle citt sicure;

Hanno dietro e dinanzi, e d'ambi i lati,

Notai, procuratori, ed avvocati.

  "Their bags were full of writs, and of citations,

Of process, and of actions and arrests,

Of bills, of answers, and of replications,

In courts of delegates, and of requests,

To grieve the simple sort with great vexations;

They had resorting to them as their guests,

Attending on their circuit, and their journeys,

Scriv'ners, and clerks, and lawyers, and attorneys."

It was what a Roman senator of the latter ages said, that their predecessors' breath stunk of garlic, but their stomachs were perfumed with a good conscience; and that, on the contrary, those of his time were all sweet odour without, but stunk within of all sorts of vices; that is to say, as I interpret it, that they abounded with learning and eloquence, but were very defective in moral honesty. Incivility, ignorance, simplicity, roughness, are the natural companions of innocence; curiosity, subtlety, knowledge, bring malice in their train; humility, fear, obedience, and affability, which are the principal things that support and maintain human society, require an empty and docile soul, and little presuming upon itself.

Christians have a particular knowledge, how natural and original an evil curiosity is in man; the thirst of knowledge, and the desire to become more wise, was the first ruin of man, and the way by which he precipitated himself into eternal damnation. Pride was his ruin and corruption. 'Tis pride that diverts him from the common path, and makes him embrace novelties, and rather choose to be head of a troop, lost and wandering in the path of error; to be a master and a teacher of lies, than to be a disciple in the school of truth, suffering himself to be led and guided by the hand of another, in the right and beaten road. 'Tis, peradventure, the meaning of this old Greek saying, that superstition follows pride, and obeys it as if it were a father: [—Greek—] Ah, presumption, how much dost thou hinder us?

After that Socrates was told that the god of wisdom had assigned to him the title of sage, he was astonished at it, and, searching and examining himself throughout, could find no foundation for this divine judgment. He knew others as just, temperate, valiant, and learned, as himself; and more eloquent, more handsome, and more profitable to their country than he. At last he concluded that he was not distinguished from others, nor wise, but only because he did not think himself so; and that his God considered the opinion of knowledge and wisdom as a singular absurdity in man; and that his best doctrine was the doctrine of ignorance, and simplicity his best wisdom. The sacred word declares those miserable among us who have an opinion of themselves: "Dust and ashes," says it to such, "what hast thou wherein to glorify thyself?" And, in another place, "God has made man like unto a shadow," of whom who can judge, when by removing the light it shall be vanished! Man is a thing of nothing.

Our force is so far from being able to comprehend the divine height, that, of the works of our Creator, those best bear his mark, and are with better title his, which we the least understand. To meet with an incredible thing is an occasion to Christians to believe; and it is so much the more according to reason, by how much it is against human reason. If it were according to reason, it would be no more a miracle; and if it were according to example, it would be no longer a singular thing. Melius scitur Deus nesdendo: "God is better known by not knowing him," says St. Austin: and Tacitus, Sanctius est ac reverentius de actis Deorum credere, quam scire; "it is more holy and reverent to believe the works of God than to know them;" and Plato thinks there is something of impiety in inquiring too curiously into God, the world, and the first causes of things: Atque illum quidem parentem hujus universitaiis invenire, difficile; et, quum jam inveneris, indicare in vulgtis, nefas: "to find out the parent of the world is very difficult; and when found out, to reveal him to the vulgar is sin," says Cicero. We talk indeed of power, truth, justice; which are words that signify some great thing; but that thing we neither see nor conceive at all. We say that God fears, that God is angry, that God loves,

   Immortalia mortali sermone notantes:

   "Giving to things immortal mortal names."

These are all agitations and emotions that cannot be in God, according to our form, nor can we imagine them, according to his. It only belongs to God to know himself, and to interpret his own works; and he does it in our language, going out of himself, to stoop to us who grovel upon the earth. How can prudence, which is the choice between good and evil, be properly attributed to him whom no evil can touch? How can reason and intelligence, which we make use of, to arrive by obscure at apparent things; seeing that nothing is obscure to him? How justice, which distributes to every one what appertains to him, a thing begot by the society and community of men, how is that in God? How temperance, which is the moderation of corporal pleasures, that have no place in the Divinity? Fortitude to support pain, labour, and dangers, as little appertains to him as the rest; these three things have no access to him. For which reason Aristotle holds him equally exempt from virtue and vice: Neque gratia, neque ira teneri potest; quod quo talia essent, imbecilla essent omnia? "He can neither be affected with favour nor indignation, because both these are the effects of frailty."

The participation we have in the knowledge of truth, such as it is, is not acquired by our own force: God has sufficiently given us to understand that, by the witnesses he has chosen out of the common people, simple and ignorant men, that he has been pleased to employ to instruct us in his admirable secrets. Our faith is not of our own acquiring; 'tis purely the gift of another's bounty: 'tis not by meditation, or by virtue of our own understanding, that we have acquired our religion, but by foreign authority and command wherein the imbecility of our own judgment does more assist us than any force of it; and our blindness more than our clearness of sight: 'tis more by__ the mediation of our ignorance than of our knowledge that we know any thing of the divine wisdom. 'Tis no wonder if our natural and earthly parts cannot conceive that supernatural and heavenly knowledge: let us bring nothing of our own, but obedience and subjection; for, as it is written, "I will destroy the wisdom of the wise, and will bring to nothing the understanding of the prudent. Where is the wise? Where is the scribe? Where is the disputer of this world? Hath not God made foolish the wisdom of this world? For after that, in the wisdom of God, the world knew not God, it pleased God by the foolishness of preaching to save them that believe."

Finally, should I examine whether it be in the power of man to find out that which he seeks and if that quest, wherein he has busied himself so many ages, has enriched him with any new force, or any solid truth; I believe he will confess, if he speaks from his conscience, that all he has got by so long inquiry is only to have learned to know his own weakness. We have only by a long study confirmed and verified the natural ignorance we were in before. The same has fallen out to men truly wise, which befalls the ears of corn; they shoot and raise their heads high and pert, whilst empty; but when full and swelled with grain in maturity, begin to flag and droop. So men, having tried and sounded all things, and having found in that mass of knowledge, and provision of so many various things, nothing solid and firm, and nothing but vanity, have quitted their presumption, and acknowledged their natural condition. 'Tis what Velleius reproaches Cotta withal and Cicero, "that they had learned of Philo, that they had learned nothing." Pherecydes, one of the seven sages, writing to Thales upon his death-bed; "I have," said he, "given order to my people, after my interment, to carry my writings to thee. If they please thee and the other sages, publish; if not, suppress them. They contain no certainty with which I myself am satisfied. Neither do I pretend to know the truth, or to attain to it. I rather open than discover things." The wisest man that ever was, being asked what he knew, made answer, "He knew this, that he knew nothing." By which he verified what has been said, that the greatest part of what we know is the least of what we do not; that is to say, that even what we think we know is but a piece, and a very little one, of our ignorance. We know things in dreams, says Plato, and are ignorant of them in truth. Ormes pene veteres nihil cognosci, nihil percipi, nihil sciri posse dixerunt; angustos sensus, imbecilles animos, brevia curricula vito. "Almost all the ancients have declared that there is nothing to be known, nothing to be perceived or understood; the senses are too limited, men's minds too weak, and the course of life too short." And of Cicero himself, who stood indebted to his learning for all he was worth, Valerius says, "That he began to disrelish letters in his old age; and when at his studies, it was with great independency upon any one party; following what he thought probable, now in one sect, and then in another, evermore wavering under the doubts of the academy." Dicendum est, sed ita ut nihil affirment, quceram omnia, dubitans plerumque, et mihi diffidens. "Something I must say, but so as to affirm nothing; I inquire into all things, but for the most part in doubt and distrust of myself."

I should have too fair a game should I consider man in his common way of living and in gross; yet I might do it by his own rule, who judges truth not by weight, but by the number of votes. Let us set the people aside,

 Qui vigilans stertit,....

 Mortua cui vita est prope jam vivo atque videnti;

 "Half of his life by lazy sleep's possess'd,

 And when awake his soul but nods at best;"

who neither feel nor judge, and let most of their natural faculties lie idle; I will take man in his highest ground. Let us consider him in that little number of men, excellent and culled out from the rest, who, having been endowed with a remarkable and particular natural force, have moreover hardened and whetted it by care, study, and art, and raised it to the highest pitch of wisdom to which it can possibly arrive. They have adjusted their souls to all ways and all biases; have propped and supported them with all foreign helps proper for them, and enriched and adorned them with all they could borrow for their advantage, both within and without the world; 'tis in these is placed the utmost and most supreme height to which human nature can attain. They have regulated the world with policies and laws. They have instructed it with arts and sciences, and by the example of their admirable manners. I shall make account of none but such men as these, their testimony and experience. Let us examine how far they have proceeded, and where they stopped. The errors and defects that we shall find amongst these men the world may boldly avow as their own.

Whoever goes in search of any thing must come to this, either to say that he has found it, or that it is not to be found, or that he is yet upon the search. All philosophy is divided into these three kinds; her design is to seek out truth, knowledge, and certainty. The Peripatetics, Epicureans, Stoics, and others, have thought they have found it. These established the sciences we have, and have treated of them as of certain knowledge. Clitomachus, Carneades, and the Academics, have despaired in their search, and concluded that truth could not be conceived by our understandings. The result of these is weakness and human ignorance. This sect has had the most and the most noble followers. Pyrrho, and other skeptics or epechists, whose dogmas are held by many of the ancients to be taken from Homer, the seven sages, and from Archilochus and Euripides, and to whose number these are added, Zeno, Democritus, and Xenophanes, say that they are yet upon the inquiry after truth. These conclude that the others, who think they have found it out, are infinitely deceived; and that it is too daring a vanity in the second sort to determine that human reason is not able to attain unto it; for this establishing a standard of our power, to know and judge the difficulty of things, is a great and extreme knowledge, of which they doubt whether man is capable:—

   Nil sciri quisquis putat, id quoque nescit,

  An sciri possit; quam se nil scire fatetur.

   "He that says nothing can be known, o'erthrows

  His own opinion, for he nothing knows,

  So knows not that."

The ignorance that knows itself, judges and condemns itself, is not an absolute ignorance; to be such, it must be ignorant of itself; so that the profession of the Pyrrhonians is to waver, doubt, and inquire, not to make themselves sure of, or responsible to themselves for any thing. Of the three actions of the soul, imaginative, appetitive, and consentive, they receive the two first; the last they kept ambiguous, without inclination or approbation, either of one thing or another, so light as it is. Zeno represented the motion of his imagination upon these divisions of the faculties of the soul thus: "An open and expanded hand signified appearance; a hand half shut, and the fingers a little bending, consent; a clenched fist, comprehension; when with the left he yet thrust the right fist closer, knowledge." Now this situation of their judgment upright and inflexible, receiving all objects without application or consent, leads them to their ataraxy, which is a peaceable condition of life, temperate, and exempt from the agitations we receive by the impression of opinion and knowledge that we think we have of things; whence spring fear, avarice, envy, immoderate desires, ambition, pride, superstition, love of novelty, rebellion, disobedience, obstinacy, and the greatest part of bodily ills; nay, and by that they are exempt from the jealousy of their discipline; for they debate after a very gentle manner; they fear no requital in their disputes; when they affirm that heavy things descend they would be sorry to be believed, and love tobe contradicted, to engender doubt and suspense of judgment, which is their end. They only put forward their propositions to contend with those they think we have in our belief. If you take their arguments, they will as readily maintain the contrary; 'tis all one to them, they have no choice. If you maintain that snow is black, they will argue on the contrary that it is white; if you say it is neither the one nor the other, they will maintain that it is both. If you hold, of certain judgment, that you know nothing, they will maintain that you do. Yea, and if by an affirmative axiom you assure them that you doubt, they will argue against you that you doubt not; or that you cannot judge and determine that you doubt. And by this extremity of doubt, which jostles itself, they separate and divide themselves from many opinions, even of those they have several ways maintained, both concerning doubt and ignorance. "Why shall not they be allowed to doubt," say they, "as well as the dogmatists, one of whom says green, another yellow? Can any thing be proposed to us to grant, or deny, which it shall not be permitted to consider as ambiguous?" And where others are carried away, either by the custom of their country, or by the instruction of parents, or by accident, as by a tempest, without judgment and without choice, nay, and for the most part before the age of discretion, to such and such an opinion, to the sect whether Stoic or Epicurean, with which they are prepossessed, enslaved, and fast bound, as to a thing they cannot forsake: Ad quamcumque disciplinant, velut tempestate, delati, ad earn, tanquam ad saxum, adhorescunt; "every one cleaves to the doctrine he has happened upon, as to a rock against which he has been thrown by tempest;" why shall not these likewise be permitted to maintain their liberty, and consider things without obligation or slavery? hoc liberiores et solutiores, quod integra illis est judicandi potestas: "in this more unconstrained and free, because they have the greater power of judging." Is it not of some advantage to be disengaged from the necessity that curbs others? Is it not better to remain in suspense than to entangle one's self in the innumerable errors that human fancy has produced? Is it not much better to suspend one's persuasion than to intermeddle with these wrangling and seditious divisions: "What shall I choose?" "What you please, provided you will choose." A very foolish answer; but such a one, nevertheless, as all dogmatism seems to point at, and by which we are not permitted to be ignorant of what we are ignorant of.

Take the most eminent side, that of the greatest reputation; it will never be so sure that you shall not be forced to attack and contend with a hundred and a hundred adversaries to defend it. Is it not better to keep out of this hurly-burly? You are permitted to embrace Aristotle's opinions of the immortality of the soul with as much zeal as your honour and life, and to give the lie to Plato thereupon, and shall they be interdicted to doubt him? If it be lawful for Pantius to maintain his opinion about augury, dreams, oracles, vaticinations, of which the Stoics made no doubt at all; why may not a wise man dare to do the same in all things that he dared to do in those he had learned of his masters, established by the common consent of the school, whereof he is a professor and a member? If it be a child that judges, he knows not what it is; if a wise man, he is prepossessed. They have reserved for themselves a marvellous advantage in battle, having eased themselves of the care of defence. If you strike them, they care not, provided they strike too, and they turn every thing to their own use. If they overcome, your argument is lame; if you, theirs; if they fall short, they verify ignorance; if you fall short, you do it; if they prove that nothing is known, 'tis well; if they cannot prove it, 'tis also well: Ut quurn in eadem re paria contrariis in partibus momenta inveniuntur, facilius ab utraque parte assertio sustineatur: "That when like sentiments happen pro and con in the same thing, the assent may on both sides be more easily suspended." And they make account to find out, with much greater facility, why a thing is false, than why 'tis true; that which is not, than that which is; and what they do not believe, than what they do. Their way of speaking is: "I assert nothing; it is no more so than so, or than neither one nor t'other; I understand it not. Appearances are everywhere equal; the law of speaking, pro or con, is the same. Nothing seems true, that may not seem false." Their sacramental word is that is to say, "I hold, I stir not." This is the burden of their song, and others of like stuff. The effect of which is a pure, entire, perfect, and absolute suspension of judgment. They make use of their reason to inquire and debate, but not to fix and determine. Whoever shall imagine a perpetual confession of ignorance, a judgment without bias, propension, or inclination, upon any occasion whatever, conceives a true idea of Pyrrhonism. I express this fancy as well as I can, by reason that many find it hard to conceive, and the authors themselves represent it a little variously and obscurely.

As to what concerns the actions of life, they are in this of the common fashion. They yield and give up themselves to their natural inclinations, to the power and impulse of passions, to the constitution of laws and customs, and to the tradition of arts; Non enim nos Deus ista scire, sed tantummodo uti, voluit. "For God would not have us know, but only use those things." They suffer their ordinary actions to be guided by those things, without any dispute or judgment. For which reason I cannot consent to what is said of Pyrrho, by those who represent him heavy and immovable, leading a kind of savage and unsociable life, standing the jostle of carts, going upon the edge of precipices, and refusing to accommodate himself to the laws. This is to enhance upon his discipline; he would never make himself a stock or a stone, he would show himself a living man, discoursing, reasoning, enjoying all reasonable conveniences and pleasures, employing and making use of all his corporal and spiritual faculties in rule and reason. The fantastic, imaginary, and false privileges that man had usurped of lording it, ordaining, and establishing, he has utterly quitted and renounced. Yet there is no sect but is constrained to permit her sage to follow several things not comprehended, perceived, or consented to, if he means to live. And if he goes to sea, he follows that design, not knowing whether his voyage shall be successful or no; and only insists upon the tightness of the vessel, the experience of the pilot, and the convenience of the season, and such probable circumstances; after which he is bound to go, and suffer himself to be governed by appearances, provided there be no express and manifest contrariety in them. He has a body, he has a soul; the senses push them, the mind spurs them on. And although he does not find in himself this proper and singular sign of judging, and that he perceives that he ought not to engage his consent, considering that there may be some false, equal to these true appearances, yet does he not, for all that, fail of carrying on the offices of his life with great liberty and convenience. How many arts are there that profess to consist more in conjecture than knowledge; that decide not on true and false, and only follow that which seems so! There are, say they, true and false, and we have in us wherewith to seek it; but not to make it stay when we touch it. We are much more prudent, in letting ourselves be regulated by the order of the world, without inquiry. A soul clear from prejudice has a marvellous advance towards tranquillity and repose. Men that judge and control their judges, do never duly submit to them.

How much more docile and easy to be governed, both by the laws of religion and civil polity, are simple and incurious minds, than those over-vigilant wits, that will still be prating of divine and human causes! There is nothing in human invention that carries so great a show of likelihood and utility as this; this presents man, naked and empty, confessing his natural weakness, fit to receive some foreign force from above, unfurnished of human, and therefore more apt to receive into him the divine knowledge, making nought of his own judgment, to give more room to faith; neither disbelieving nor establishing any dogma against common observances; humble, obedient, disciplinable, and studious; a sworn enemy of heresy; and consequently freeing himself from vain and irreligious opinions, introduced by false sects. 'Tis a blank paper prepared to receive such forms from the finger of God as he shall please to write upon it. The more we resign and commit ourselves to God, and the more we renounce ourselves, of the greater value we are. "Take in good part," says Ecclesiastes, "the things that present themselves to thee, as they seem and taste from hand to mouth; the rest is out of thy knowledge." Dominus novit cogitationes hominum, quoniam van sunt: "The Lord knoweth the hearts of men, that they are but vanity."

Thus we see that of the three general sects of philosophy, two make open profession of doubt and ignorance; and in that of the Dogmatists, which is the third, it is easy to discover that the greatest part of them only assume this face of confidence and assurance that

they may produce the better effect; they have not so much thought to establish any certainty for us, as to show us how far they have proceeded in their search of truth: Quam docti jingunt magis quam nrunt: "Which the learned rather feign than know." Timus, being to instruct Socrates in what he knew of the gods, the world, and men, proposes to speak to him as a man to a man; and that it is sufficient, if his reasons are probable as those of another; for that exact reasons were neither in his nor any other mortal hand; which one of his followers has thus imitated: Ut potero, explicabo: nec tamen, ut Pythius Apollo, certa ut sint et fixa qu dixero; sed, ut homunculus, probabilia conjectur sequens: "I will, as well as I am able, explain; affirming, yet not as the Pythian oracle, that what I say is fixed and certain, but like a mere man, that follows probabilities by conjecture." And this, upon the natural and common subject of the contempt of death; he has elsewhere translated from the very words of Plato: Si forte, de Deorum natur ortuque mundi disserentes, minus id quod habemiis in animo consequi-mur, haud erit mirum; oquum est enim meminisse, et me, qui disseram, hominem esse, et vos, qui judicetis, ut, si probabilia dicentur, nihil ultra requiratis? "If perchance, when we discourse of the nature of God, and the world's original, we cannot do it as we desire, it will be no great wonder. For it is just you should remember that both I who speak and you who are to judge, are men; so that if probable things are delivered, you shall require and expect no more." Aristotle ordinarily heaps up a great number of other men's opinions and beliefs, to compare them with his own, and to let us see how much he has gone beyond them, and how much nearer he approaches to the likelihood of truth; for truth is not to be judged by the authority and testimony of others; which made Epicurus religiously avoid quoting them in his writings. This is the prince of all dogmatists, and yet we are told by him that the more we know the more we have room for doubt. In earnest, we sometimes see him shroud and muffle up himself in so thick and so inextricable an obscurity that we know not what to make of his advice; it is, in effect, a Pyrrhonism under a resolutive form. Hear Cicero's protestation, who expounds to us another's fancy by his own: Qui requirunt quid de quque re ipsi sentiamus, curiosius id faciunt quam necesse est,.... Hoc in philosophi ratio, contra omnia disserendi, nuttamque rem aperte judicandi, profecta a Socrate, repetita ab Arcesila, conjirmata a Gameade, usqu ad nostram viget cetatem..........Hi sumus, qui omnibus veris falsa quodam adjuncta esse dicamus, tanta similitudine, ut in iis nulla insit certe judicandi et assentiendi nota. "They who desire to know what we think of every thing are therein more inquisitive than is necessary. This practice in philosophy of disputing against every thing, and of absolutely concluding nothing, begun by Socrates, repeated by Arcesilaus, and confirmed by Cameades, has continued in use even to our own times. We are they who declare that there is so great a mixture of things false amongst all that are true, and they so resemble one another, that there can be in them no certain mark to direct us either to judge or assent." Why hath not Aristotle only, but most of the philosophers, affected difficulty, if not to set a greater value upon the vanity of the subject, and amuse the curiosity of our minds by giving them this hollow and fleshless bone to pick? Clitomachus affirmed "That he could never discover by Carneades's writings what opinion he was of." This was it that made Epicurus affect to be abstruse, and that procured Heraclitus the epithet of [—Greek—] Difficulty is a coin the learned make use of, like jugglers, to conceal the vanity of their art, and which human sottishness easily takes for current pay.

Claras, ob obscuram linguam, magis inter manes...

Omnia enim stolidi magis admirantur amantque

Inversis qu sub verbis latitantia cemunt.

"Bombast and riddle best do puppies please,

For fools admire and love such things as these;

And a dull quibble, wrapt in dubious phrase,

Up to the height doth their wise wonder raise."

Cicero reprehends some of his friends for giving more of their time to the study of astrology, logic, and geometry, than they were really worth; saying that they were by these diverted from the duties of life, and more profitable and proper studies. The Cyrenaick philosophers, in like manner, despised physics and logic. Zeno, in the very beginning of the books of the commonwealth, declared all the liberal arts of no use. Chrysippus said "That what Plato and Aristotle had writ, concerning logic, they had only done in sport, and by way of exercise;" and could not believe that they spoke in earnest of so vain a thing. Plutarch says the same of metaphysics. And Epicurus would have said as much of rhetoric, grammar, poetry, mathematics, and, natural philosophy excepted, of all the sciences; and Socrates of them all, excepting that which treats of manners and of life. Whatever any one required to be instructed in, by him, he would ever, in the first place, demand an account of the conditions of his life present and past, which he examined and judged, esteeming all other learning subsequent to that and supernumerary: Parum mihi placeant e littero quo ad virtutem doctoribus nihil pro-fuerunt. "That learning is in small repute with me which nothing profited the teachers themselves to virtue." Most of the arts have been in like manner decried by the same knowledge; but they did not consider that it was from the purpose to exercise their wits in those very matters wherein there was no solid advantage.

As to the rest, some have looked upon Plato as a dogmatist, others as a doubter, others in some things the one, and in other things the other. Socrates, the conductor of his dialogues, is eternally upon questions and stirring up disputes, never determining, never satisfying, and professes to have no other science but that of opposing himself. Homer, their author, has equally laid the foundations of all the sects of philosophy, to show how indifferent it was which way we should choose. 'Tis said that ten several sects sprung from Plato; yet, in my opinion, never did any instruction halt and stumble, if his does not.

Socrates said that midwives, in taking upon them the trade of helping others to bring forth, left the trade of bringing forth themselves; and that by the title of a wise man or sage, which the gods had conferred upon him, he was disabled, in his virile and mental love, of the faculty of bringing forth, contenting himself to help and assist those that could; to open their nature, anoint the passes, and facilitate their birth; to judge of the infant, baptize, nourish, fortify, swath, and circumcise it, exercising and employing his understanding in the perils and fortunes of others.

It is so with the most part of this third sort of authors, as the ancients have observed in the writings of Anaxagoras, Democritus, Parmenides, Xenophanes, and others. They have a way of writing, doubtful in substance and design, rather inquiring than teaching, though they mix their style with some dogmatical periods. Is not the same thing seen in Seneca and Plutarch? How many contradictions are there to be found if a man pry narrowly into them! So many that the reconciling lawyers ought first to reconcile them every one to themselves. Plato seems to have affected this method of philosophizing in dialogues; to the end that he might with greater decency, from several mouths, deliver the diversity and variety of his own fancies. It is as well to treat variously of things as to treat of them conformably, and better, that is to say, more copiously and with greater profit. Let us take example from ourselves: judgments are the utmost point of all dogmatical and determinative speaking; and yet those arrets that our parliaments give the people, the most exemplary of them, and those most proper to nourish in them the reverence due to that dignity, principally through the sufficiency of the persons acting, derive their beauty not so much from the conclusion, which with them is quotidian and common to every judge, as from the dispute and heat of divers and contrary arguments that the matter of law and equity will permit And the largest field for reprehension that some philosophers have against others is drawn from the diversities and contradictions wherein every one of them finds himself perplexed, either on purpose to show the vacillation of the human mind concerning every thing, or ignorantly compelled by the volubility and incomprehensibility of all matter; which is the meaning of the maxim—"In a slippery and sliding place let us suspend our belief;" for, as Euripides says,—

"God's various works perplex the thoughts of men."

Like that which Empedocles, as if transported with a divine fury, and compelled by truth, often strewed here and there in his writings: "No, no, we feel nothing, we see nothing; all things are concealed from us; there is not one thing of which we can positively say what it is;" according to the divine saying: Cogitationes mortalium timid, et incert adinventiones nostro et providentice. "For the thoughts of mortal men are doubtful; and our devices are but uncertain." It is not to be thought strange if men, despairing to overtake what they hunt after, have not however lost the pleasure of the chase; study being of itself so pleasant an employment; and so pleasant that amongst the pleasures, the Stoics forbid that also which proceeds from the exercise of the mind, will have it curbed, and find a kind of intemperance in too much knowledge.

Democritus having eaten figs at his table that tasted of honey, fell presently to considering with himself whence they should derive this unusual sweetness; and to be satisfied in it, was about to rise from the table to see the place whence the figs had been gathered; which his maid observing, and having understood the cause, smilingly told him that "he need not trouble himself about that, for she had put them into a vessel in which there had been honey." He was vexed at this discovery, and that she had deprived him of the occasion of this inquiry, and robbed his curiosity of matter to work upon: "Go thy way," said he, "thou hast done me an injury; but, for all that, I will seek out the cause as if it were natural;" and would willingly have found out some true reason for a false and imaginary effect. This story of a famous and great philosopher very clearly represents to us that studious passion that puts us upon the pursuit of things, of the acquisition of which we despair. Plutarch gives a like example of some one who would not be satisfied in that whereof he was in doubt, that he might not lose the pleasure of inquiring into it; like the other who would not that his physician should allay the thirst of his fever, that he might not lose the pleasure of quenching it by drinking. Satius est supervacua discere, quam nihil. "'Tis better to learn more than necessary than nothing at all." As in all sorts of feeding, the pleasure of eating is very often single and alone, and that what we take, which is acceptable to the palate, is not always nourishing or wholesome; so that which our minds extract from science does not cease to be pleasant, though there be nothing in it either nutritive or healthful. Thus they say: "The consideration of nature is a diet proper for our minds, it raises and elevates us, makes us disdain low and terrestrial things, by comparing them with those that are celestial and high. The mere inquisition into great and occult things is very pleasant, even to those who acquire no other benefit than the reverence and fear of judging it." This is what they profess. The vain image of this sickly curiosity is yet more manifest in this other example which they so often urge. "Eudoxus wished and begged of the gods that he might once see the sun near at hand, to comprehend the form, greatness, and beauty of it; even though he should thereby be immediately burned." He would at the price of his life purchase a knowledge, of which the use and possession should at the same time be taken from him; and for this sudden and vanishing knowledge lose all the other knowledge he had in present, or might afterwards have acquired.

I cannot easily persuade myself that Epicurus, Plato, and Pytagoras, have given us their atom, idea and numbers, for current pay. They were too wise to establish their articles of faith upon things so disputable and uncertain. But in that obscurity and ignorance in which the world then was, every one of these great men endeavoured to present some kind of image or reflection of light, and worked their brains for inventions that might have a pleasant and subtle appearance; provided that, though false, they might make good their ground against those that would oppose them. Unicuique ista pro ingenio finguntur, non ex scienti vi. "These things every one fancies according to his wit, and not by any power of knowledge."

One of the ancients, who was reproached, "That he professed philosophy, of which he nevertheless in his own judgment made no great account," made answer, "That this was truly to philosophize."

They wished to consider all, to balance every thing, and found that an employment well suited to our natural curiosity. Some things they wrote for the benefit of public society, as their religions; and for that consideration it was but reasonable that they should not examine public opinions to the quick, that they might not disturb the common obedience to the laws and customs of their country.

Plato treats of this mystery with a raillery manifest enough; for where he writes according to his own method he gives no certain rule. When he plays the legislator he borrows a magisterial and positive style, and boldly there foists in his most fantastic inventions, as fit to persuade the vulgar, as impossible to be believed by himself; knowing very well how fit we are to receive all sorts of impressions, especially the most immoderate and preposterous; and yet, in his Laws, he takes singular care that nothing be sung in public but poetry, of which the fiction and fabulous relations tend to some advantageous end; it being so easy to imprint all sorts of phantasms in human minds, that it were injustice not to feed them rather with profitable untruths than with untruths that are unprofitable and hurtful. He says very roundly, in his Republic, "That it is often necessary, for the benefit of men, to deceive them." It is very easy to distinguish that some of the sects have more followed truth, and the others utility, by which the last have gained their reputation. 'Tis the misery of our condition that often that which presents itself to our imagination for the truest does not appear the most useful to life. The boldest sects, as the Epicurean, Pyrrhonian, and the new Academic, are yet constrained to submit to the civil law at the end of the account.

There are other subjects that they have tumbled and tossed about, some to the right and others to the left, every one endeavouring, right or wrong, to give them some kind of colour; for, having found nothing so abstruse that they would not venture to speak of, they are very often forced to forge weak and ridiculous conjectures; not that they themselves looked upon them as any foundation, or establishing any certain truth, but merely for exercise. Non tam id sensisse quod dicerent, quam exercere ingnia materio difficultate videntur voluisse. "They seem not so much themselves to have believed what they said, as to have had a mind to exercise their wits in the difficulty of the matter." And if we did not take it thus, how should we palliate so great inconstancy, variety, and vanity of opinions, as we see have been produced by those excellent and admirable men? As, for example, what can be more vain than to imagine, to guess at God, by our analogies and conjectures? To direct and govern him and the world by our capacities and our laws? And to serve ourselves, at the expense of the divinity, with what small portion of capacity he has been pleased to impart to our natural condition; and because we cannot extend our sight to his glorious throne, to have brought him down to our corruption and our miseries?

Of all human and ancient opinions concerning religion, that seems to me the most likely and most excusable, that acknowledged God as an incomprehensible power, the original and preserver of all things, all goodness, all perfection, receiving and taking in good part the honour and reverence that man paid him, under what method, name, or ceremonies soever—

    Jupiter omnipotens, rerum, regumque, demque,

    Progenitor, genitrixque.

> "Jove, the almighty, author of all things,
>
> The father, mother, of both gods and kings."

This zeal has universally been looked upon from heaven with a gracious eye. All governments have reaped fruit from their devotion; impious men and actions have everywhere had suitable events. Pagan histories acknowledge dignity, order, justice, prodigies, and oracles, employed for their profit and instruction in their fabulous religions; God, through his mercy, vouchsafing, by these temporal benefits, to cherish the tender principles of a kind of brutish knowledge that natural reason gave them of him, through the deceiving images of their dreams. Not only deceiving and false, but impious also and injurious, are those that man has forged from his own invention: and of all the religions that St. Paul found in repute at Athens, that which they had dedicated "to the unknown God" seemed to him the most to be excused.

Pythagoras shadowed the truth a little more closely, judging that the knowledge of this first cause and being of beings ought to be indefinite, without limitation, without declaration; that it was nothing else than the extreme effort of our imagination towards perfection, every one amplifying the idea according to the talent of his capacity. But if Numa attempted to conform the devotion of his people to this project; to attach them to a religion purely mental, without any prefixed object and material mixture, he undertook a thing of no use; the human mind could never support itself floating in such an infinity of inform thoughts; there is required some certain image to be presented according to its own model. The divine majesty has thus, in some sort, suffered himself to be circumscribed in corporal limits for our advantage. His supernatural and celestial sacraments have signs of our earthly condition; his adoration is by sensible offices and words; for 'tis man that believes and prays. I shall omit the other arguments upon this subject; but a man would have much ado to make me believe that the sight of our crucifixes, that the picture of our Saviour's passion, that the ornaments and ceremonious motions of our churches, that the voices accommodated to the devotion of our thoughts, and that emotion of the senses, do not warm the souls of the people with a religious passion of very advantageous effect.

Of those to whom they have given a body, as necessity required in that universal blindness, I should, I fancy, most incline to those who adored the sun:—

> La Lumire commune,
>
> L'oil du monde; et si Dieu au chef porte des yeux,
>
> Les rayons du soleil sont ses yeulx radieux,
>
> Qui donnent vie touts, nous maintiennent et gardent,

Et les faictsdes humains en ce monde regardent:

Ce beau, ce grand soleil qui nous faict les saisons,

Selon qu'il entre ou sort de ses douze maisons;

Qui remplit l'univers de ses vertus cognues;

Qui d'un traict de ses yeulx nous dissipe les nues;

L'esprit, l'ame du monde, ardent et flamboyant,

En la course d'un jour tout le Ciel tournoyant;

Plein d'immense grandeur, rond, vagabond, et ferme;

Lequel tient dessoubs luy tout le monde pour terme:

En repos, sans repos; oysif, et sans sjour;

Fils aisn de nature, et le pre du jour:

"The common light that equal shines on all,

Diffused around the whole terrestrial ball;

And, if the almighty Ruler of the skies

Has eyes, the sunbeams are his radiant eyes,

That life and safety give to young and old,

And all men's actions upon earth behold.

This great, this beautiful, the glorious sun,

Who makes their course the varied seasons run;

That with his virtues fills the universe,

And with one glance can sullen clouds disperse;

Earth's life and soul, that, flaming in his sphere,

Surrounds the heavens in one day's career;

Immensely great, moving yet firm and round,

Who the whole world below has made his bound;

At rest, without rest, idle without stay,

Nature's first son, and father of the day:"

forasmuch as, beside this grandeur and beauty of his, 'tis the only piece of this machine that we discover at the remotest distance from us; and by that means so little known that they were pardonable for entering into so great admiration and reverence of it.

Thales, who first inquired into this sort of matter, believed God to be a Spirit that made all things of water; Anaximander, that the gods were always dying and entering into life again; and that there were an infinite number of worlds; Anaximines, that the air was God, that he was procreate and immense, always moving. Anaxagoras the first, was of opinion that the description and manner of all things were conducted by the power and reason of an infinite spirit. Alcmon gave divinity to the sun, moon, and stars, and to the soul. Pythagoras made God a spirit, spread over the nature of all things, whence our souls are extracted; Parmenides, a circle surrounding the heaven, and supporting the world by the ardour of light. Empedocles pronounced the four elements, of which all things are composed, to be gods; Protagoras had nothing to say, whether they were or were not, or what they were; Democritus was one while of opinion that the images and their circuitions were gods; another while, the nature that darts out those images; and then, our science and intelligence. Plato divides his belief into several opinions; he says, in his Timus, that the Father of the World cannot be named; in his Laws, that men are not to inquire into his being; and elsewhere, in the very same books, he makes the world, the heavens, the stars, the earth, and our souls, gods; admitting, moreover, those which have been received by ancient institution in every republic.

Xenophon reports a like perplexity in Socrates's doctrine; one while that men are not to inquire into the form of God, and presently makes him maintain that the sun is God, and the soul God; that there is but one God, and then that there are many. Speusippus, the nephew of Plato, makes God a certain power governing all things, and that he has a soul. Aristotle one while says it is the spirit, and another the world; one while he gives the world another master, and another while makes God the heat of heaven. Zenocrates makes eight, five named amongst the planets; the sixth composed of all the fixed stars, as of so many members; the seventh and eighth, the sun and moon. Heraclides Ponticus does nothing but float in his opinion, and finally deprives God of sense, and makes him shift from one form to another, and at last says that it is heaven and earth. Theophrastus wanders in the same irresolution amongst his fancies, attributing the superintendency of the world one while to the understanding, another while to heaven, and then to the stars. Strato says that 'tis nature, she having the power of generation, augmentation, and diminution, without form and sentiment Zeno says 'tis the law of nature, commanding good and prohibiting evil; which law is an animal; and takes away the accustomed gods, Jupiter, Juno, and Vesta. Diogenes Apolloniates, that 'tis air. Zenophanes makes God round, seeing and hearing, not breathing, and having nothing in common with human nature. Aristo thinks the form of God to be incomprehensible, deprives him of sense, and knows not whether he be an animal or something else; Cleanthes, one while supposes it to be reason, another while the world, another the soul of nature, and then the supreme heat rolling about, and environing all. Perseus, Zeno's disciple, was of opinion that men have given the title of gods to such as have been useful, and have added any notable advantage to human life, and even to profitable things themselves. Chrysippus made a confused heap of all the preceding theories, and reckons, amongst a thousand forms of gods that he makes, the men also that have been deified. Diagoras and Theodoras flatly denied that there were any gods at all. Epicurus makes the gods shining, transparent, and perflable, lodged as betwixt two forts, betwixt two worlds, secure from blows, clothed in a human figure, and with such members as we have; which members are to them of no use:—

> Ego Deum genus esse semper duxi, et dicam colitum;

> Sed eos non curare opinor quid agat humanum genus.

> "I ever thought that gods above there were,

> But do not think they care what men do here."

Trust to your philosophy, my masters; and brag that you have found the bean in the cake when you see what a rattle is here with so many philosophical heads! The perplexity of so many worldly forms has gained this over me, that manners and opinions contrary to mine do not so much displease as instruct me; nor so much make me proud as they humble me, in comparing them. And all other choice than what comes from the express and immediate hand of God seems to me a choice of very little privilege. The policies of the world are no less opposite upon this subject than the schools, by which we may understand that fortune itself is not more variable and inconstant, nor more blind and inconsiderate, than our reason. The things that are most unknown are most proper to be deified; wherefore to make gods of ourselves, as the ancients did, exceeds the extremest weakness of understanding. I would much rather have gone along with those who adored the serpent, the dog, or the ox; forasmuch as their nature and being is less known to us, and that we have more room to imagine what we please of those beasts, and to attribute to them extraordinary faculties. But to have made gods of our own condition, of whom we ought to know the imperfections; and to have attributed to them desire, anger, revenge, marriages, generation, alliances, love, jealousy, our members and bones, our fevers and pleasures, our death and obsequies; this must needs have proceeded from a marvellous inebriety of the human understanding;

> Qu procul usque adeo divino ab numine distant,

> Inque Dem numro qu sint indigna videri;

"From divine natures these so distant are,

They are unworthy of that character."

Formo, otates, vestitus, omatus noti sunt; genera, conjugia, cognationes, omniaque traducta ad similitudinem imbellitar tis humano: nam et perturbatis animis inducuntur; accipimus enim deorurn cupiditates, cegritudines, iracundias; "Their forms, ages, clothes, and ornaments are known: their descents, marriages, and kindred, and all adapted to the similitude of human weakness; for they are represented to us with anxious minds, and we read of the lusts, sickness, and anger of the gods;" as having attributed divinity not only to faith, virtue, honour, concord, liberty, victory, and piety; but also to voluptuousness, fraud, death, envy, old age, misery; to fear, fever, ill fortune, and other injuries of our frail and transitory life:—

Quid juvat hoc, templis nostros inducere mores?

O curv in terris anim et colestium inanes!

"O earth-born souls! by earth-born passions led,

To every spark of heav'nly influence dead!

Think ye that what man values will inspire

In minds celestial the same base desire?"

The Egyptians, with an impudent prudence, interdicted, upon pain of hanging, that any one should say that their gods, Serapis and Isis, had formerly been men; and yet no one was ignorant that they had been such; and their effigies, represented with the finger upon the mouth, signified, says Varro, that mysterious decree to their priests, to conceal their mortal original, as it must by necessary consequence cancel all the veneration paid to them. Seeing that man so much desired to equal himself to God, he had done better, says Cicero, to have attracted those divine conditions to himself, and drawn them down hither below, than to send his corruption and misery up on high; but, to take it right, he has several ways done both the one and the other, with like vanity of opinion.

When philosophers search narrowly into the hierarchy of their gods, and make a great bustle about distinguishing their alliances, offices, and power, I cannot believe they speak as they think. When Plato describes Pluto's orchard to us, and the bodily conveniences or pains that attend us after the ruin and annihilation of our bodies, and accommodates them to the feeling we have in this life:—

   Secreti celant calles, et myrtea circum

   Sylva tegit; cur non ips in morte relinquunt;

   "In secret vales and myrtle groves they lie,

   Nor do cares leave them even when they die."

when Mahomet promises his followers a Paradise hung with tapestry, gilded and enamelled with gold and precious stones, furnished with wenches of excelling beauty, rare wines, and delicate dishes; it is easily discerned that these are deceivers that accommodate their promises to our sensuality, to attract and allure us by hopes and opinions suitable to our mortal appetites. And yet some amongst us are fallen into the like error, promising to themselves after the resurrection a terrestrial and temporal life, accompanied with all sorts of worldly conveniences and pleasures. Can we believe that Plato, he who had such heavenly conceptions, and was so well acquainted with the Divinity as thence to derive the name of the Divine Plato, ever thought that the poor creature, man, had any thing in him applicable to that incomprehensible power? and that he believed that the weak holds we are able to take were capable, or the force of our understanding sufficient, to participate of beatitude or eternal pains? We should then tell him from human reason: "If the pleasures thou dost promise us in the other life are of the same kind that I have enjoyed here below, this has nothing in common with infinity; though all my five natural senses should be even loaded with pleasure, and my soul full of all the contentment it could hope or desire, we know what all this amounts to, all this would be nothing; if there be any thing of mine there, there is nothing divine; if this be no more than what may belong to our present condition, it cannot be of any value. All contentment of mortals is mortal. Even the knowledge of our parents, children, and friends, if that can affect and delight us in the other world, if that still continues a satisfaction to us there, we still remain in earthly and finite conveniences. We cannot as we ought conceive the greatness of these high and divine promises, if we could in any sort conceive them; to have a worthy imagination of them we must imagine them unimaginable, inexplicable, and incomprehensible, and absolutely another thing than those of our miserable experience." "Eye hath not seen," saith St. Paul, "nor ear heard, neither hath entered into the heart of man, the things that God hath prepared for them that love him." And if, to render us capable, our being were reformed and changed (as thou, Plato, sayest, by thy purifications), it ought to be so extreme and total a change, that by physical doctrine it be no more us;—

   Hector erat tunc cum bello certabat; at ille

Tractus ab monio non erat Hector eqao;

He Hector was whilst he could fight, but when

Dragg'd by Achilles' steeds, no Hector then;

it must be something else that must receive these recompenses:—

Quod mutatur... dissolvitur; interit ergo;

Trajiciuntur enim partes, atque ordine migrant.

"Things changed dissolved are, and therefore die;

Their parts are mix'd, and from their order fly."

For in Pythagoras's metempsychosis, and the change of habitation that he imagined in souls, can we believe that the lion, in whom the soul of Csar is enclosed, does espouse Csar's passions, or that the lion is he? For if it was still Csar, they would be in the right who, controverting this opinion with Plato, reproach him that the son might be seen to ride his mother transformed into a mule, and the like absurdities. And can we believe that in the mutations that are made of the bodies of animals into others of the same kind, the new comers are not other than their predecessors? From the ashes of a phoenix, a worm, they say, is engendered, and from that another phoenix; who can imagine that this second phoenix is no other than the first? We see our silk-worms, as it were, die and wither; and from this withered body a butterfly is produced; and from that another worm; how ridiculous would it be to imagine that this was still the first! That which once has ceased to be is no more:—

Nec, si materiam nostram collegerit tas

Post obitum, rursumque redegerit, ut sita nunc est,

Atque iterum nobis fuerint data lumina vit,

Pertineat quidquam tamen ad nos id quoque factum,

Interrupta semel cum sit repetentia nostra.

"Neither tho' time should gather and restore

Our matter to the form it was before,

And give again new light to see withal,

Would that new figure us concern at all;

Or we again ever the same be seen,

Our being having interrupted been."

And, Plato, when thou sayest in another place that it shall be the spiritual part of man that will be concerned in the fruition of the recompense of another life, thou tellest us a thing wherein there is as little appearance of truth:—

Scilicet, avolsis radicibus, ut nequit ullam

Dispicere ipsa oculus rem, seorsum corpore toto;

"No more than eyes once from their optics torn,

Can ever after any thing discern;"

for, by this account, it would no more be man, nor consequently us, who would be concerned in this enjoyment; for we are composed of two principal essential parts, the separation of which is the death and ruin of our being:—

Inter enim jecta est vital pausa, vageque

Deerrarunt passim motus ab sensibus omnes;

"When once that pause of life is come between,

'Tis just the same as we had never been;"

we cannot say that the man suffers when the worms feed upon his members, and that the earth consumes them:—

Et nihil hoc ad nos, qui coltu conjugioque

Corporis atque anim consistimus uniter apti.

"What's that to us? for we are only we,

While soul and body in one frame agree."

Moreover, upon what foundation of their justice can the gods take notice of or reward man after his death and virtuous actions, since it was themselves that put them in the way and mind to do them? And why should they be offended at or punish him for wicked ones, since themselves have created in him so frail a condition, and when, with one glance of their will, they might prevent him from falling? Might not Epicurus, with great colour of human reason, object this to Plato, did he not often save himself with this sentence: "That it is impossible to establish any thing certain of the immortal nature by the mortal?" She does nothing but err throughout, but especially when she meddles with divine things. Who does more evidently perceive this than we? For although we have given her certain and infallible principles; and though we have enlightened her steps with the sacred lamp of truth that it has pleased God to communicate to us; we daily see, nevertheless, that if she swerve never so little from the ordinary path; and that she stray from, or wander out of the way set out and beaten by the church, how soon she loses, confounds and fetters herself, tumbling and floating in this vast, turbulent, and waving sea of human opinions, without restraint, and without any determinate end; so soon as she loses that great and common road, she enters into a labyrinth of a thousand several paths.

Man cannot be any thing but what he is, nor imagine beyond the reach of his capacity. "Tis a greater presumption," says Plutarch, "in them who are but men to attempt to speak and discourse of the gods and demi-gods than it is in a man utterly ignorant of music to give an opinion of singing; or in a man who never saw a camp to dispute about arms and martial affairs, presuming by some light conjecture to understand the effects of an art he is totally a stranger to." Antiquity, I believe, thought to put a compliment upon, and to add something to, the divine grandeur in assimilating it to man, investing it with his faculties, and adorning it with his ugly humours and most shameful necessities; offering it our aliments to eat, presenting it with our dances, mummeries, and farces, to divert it; with our vestments to cover it, and our houses to inhabit, coaxing it with the odour of incense and the sounds of music, with festoons and nosegays; and to accommodate it to our vicious passions, flattering its justice with inhuman vengeance, and with the ruin and dissipation of things by it created and preserved as Tiberius Sempronius, who burnt the rich spoils and arms he had gained from the enemy in Sardinia for a sacrifice to Vulcan; and Paulus milius, those of Macedonia, to Mars and Minerva; and Alexander, arriving at the Indian Ocean, threw several great vessels of gold into the sea, in honour of Thetes; and moreover loading her altars with a slaughter not of innocent beasts only, but of men also, as several nations, and ours among the rest, were commonly used to do; and I believe there is no nation under the sun that has not done the same:—

Sulmone creatos

> Quatuor hc juvenes, totidem quos educat Ufens,
>
> Viventes rapit, inferias quos immolet umbris.

> "Four sons of Sulmo, four whom Ufens bred,
>
> He took in flight, and living victims led,
>
> To please the ghost of Pallas, and expire
>
> In sacrifice before his fun'ral pyre."

The Get hold themselves to be immortal, and that their death is nothing but a journey to their god Zamolxis. Every five years they dispatch some one among them to him, to entreat of him such necessaries as they stand in need of. This envoy is chosen by lot, and the form of dispatching him, after he has been instructed by word of mouth what he is to deliver, is that of the assistants, three hold up as many javelins, upon which the rest throw his body with all their force. If he happen to be wounded in a mortal part, and that he immediately dies, 'tis held a certain argument of divine favour; but if he escapes, he is looked upon as a wicked and execrable wretch, and another is dismissed after the same manner in his stead. Amestris, the mother of Xerxes, being grown old, caused at once fourteen young men, of the best families of Persia, to be buried alive, according to the religion of the country, to gratify some infernal deity. And even to this day the idols of Themixtitan are cemented with the blood of little children, and they delight in no sacrifice but of these pure and infantine souls; a justice thirsty of innocent blood:—

> Tantum religio potuit suadere maloram.

> "Such impious use was of religion made,
>
> So many demon acts it could persuade."

The Carthaginians immolated their own children to Saturn; and those who had none of their own bought of others, the father and mother being in the mean time obliged to assist at the ceremony with a gay and contented countenance.

It was a strange fancy to think to gratify the divine bounty with our afflictions; like the Lacedemonians, who regaled their Diana with the tormenting of young boys, whom they caused to be whipped for her sake, very often to death. It was a savage humour to imagine to gratify the architect by the subversion of his building, and to think to take away the punishment due to the guilty by punishing the innocent; and that poor Iphigenia, at the port of Aulis, should by her death and immolation acquit, towards God, the whole army of the Greeks from all the crimes they had committed;

Et casta inceste, nubendi tempore in ipso,

Hostia concideret mactatu mosta parentis;

"That the chaste virgin in her nuptial band

Should die by an unnat'ral father's hand;"

and that the two noble and generous souls of the two Decii, the father and the son, to incline the favour of the gods to be propitious to the affairs of Rome, should throw themselves headlong into the thickest of the enemy: Quo fuit tanta deorum iniquitas, ut placari populo Romano non possent, nisi tales viri occidissent? "How great an injustice in the gods was it that they could not be reconciled to the people of Rome unless such men perished!" To which may be added, that it is not for the criminal to cause himself to be scourged according to his own measure nor at his own time, but that it purely belongs to the judge, who considers nothing as chastisements but the penalty that he appoints, and cannot call that punishment which proceeds from the consent of him that suffers. The divine vengeance presupposes an absolute dissent in us, both for its justice and for our own penalty. And therefore it was a ridiculous humour of Polycrates, tyrant of Samos, who, to interrupt the continued course of his good fortune, and to balance it, went and threw the dearest and most precious jewel he had into the sea, believing that by this voluntary and antedated mishap he bribed and satisfied the revolution and vicissitude of fortune; and she, to mock his folly, ordered it so that the same jewel came again into his hands, found in the belly of a fish. And then to what end were those tearings and dismemberments of the Corybantes, the Menades, and, in our times, of the Mahometans, who slash their faces, bosoms, and limbs, to gratify their prophet; seeing that the offence lies in the will, not in the breast, eyes, genitals, roundness of form, the shoulders, or the throat? Tantus est perturbto mentis, et sedibus suis pilso, furor, ut sic dii placentur, quemadmodum ne homines quidem soviunt. "So great is the fury and madness of troubled minds when once displaced from the seat of reason, as if the gods should be appeased with what even men are not so cruel as to approve." The use of this natural contexture has not only respect to us, but also to the service of God and other men; 'tis as unjust for us voluntarily to wound or hurt it as to kill ourselves upon any pretence whatever; it seems to be great cowardice and treason to exercise cruelty upon, and to destroy, the functions of the body that are stupid and servile, to spare the soul the solicitude of governing them according to reason: Ubi iratos deos timent, qui sic propitios habere merentur? In regi libidinis voluptatem castrati sunt quidam; sed nemo sibi, ne vir esset, jubente domino, mantis intulit. "Where are they so afraid of the anger of the gods as to merit their favour at that rate? Some, indeed, have been made eunuchs for the lust of princes: but no man at his master's command has put his own hand to unman himself." So did they fill their religion with several ill effects:—

Spius olim Religio peperit scelerosa atque impia facta.

"In elder times Religion did commit most fearful crimes."

Now nothing of ours can in any sort be compared or likened unto the divine nature, which will not blemish and stain it with much imperfection.

How can that infinite beauty, power, and goodness, admit of any correspondence or similitude to such abject things as we are, without extreme wrong and manifest dishonour to his divine greatness? Infirmum dei fortius est hominibs; et stultum dei sapientius est hominibus. "For the foolishness of God is wiser than men, and the weakness of God is stronger than men." Stilpo, the philosopher, being asked, "Whether the gods were delighted with our adorations and sacrifices?"—"You are indiscreet," answered he; "let us withdraw apart, if you would talk of such things." Nevertheless, we prescribe him bounds, we keep his power besieged by our reasons (I call our ravings and dreams reason, with the dispensation of philosophy, which says, "That the wicked man, and even the fool, go mad by reason, but a particular form of reason"), we would subject him to the vain and feeble appearances of our understandings,—him who has made both us and our knowledge. Because that nothing is made of nothing, God therefore could not make the world without matter. What! has God put into our hands the keys and most secret springs of his power? Is he obliged not to exceed the limits of our knowledge? Put the case, O man! that thou hast been able here to mark some footsteps of his effects; dost thou therefore think that he has employed all he can, and has crowded all his forms and ideas in this work? Thou seest nothing but the order and revolution of this little cave in which thou art lodged, if, indeed, thou dost see so much; whereas his divinity has an infinite jurisdiction beyond. This part is nothing in comparison of the whole:—

   Omnia cum colo, terrque, manque,

Nil sunt ad summam summal totius omnem.

   "The earth, the sea, and skies, from pole to pole,

   Are small, nay, nothing to the mighty whole."

'Tis a municipal law that thou allegest, thou knowest not what is universal Tie thyself to that to which thou art subject, but not him; he is not of thy brotherhood, thy fellow-citizen, or companion. If he has in some sort communicated himself unto thee, 'tis not to debase himself unto thy littleness, nor to make thee comptroller of his power; the human body cannot fly to the clouds; rules are for thee. The sun runs every day his ordinary course; the bounds of the sea and the earth cannot be confounded; the water is unstable and without firmness; a wall, unless it be broken, is impenetrable to a solid body; a man cannot preserve his life in the flames; he cannot be both in heaven and upon earth, and corporally in a thousand places at once. 'Tis for thee that he has made these rules; 'tis thee that they concern; he has manifested to Christians that he has enfranchised himself from them all when it pleased him. And, in truth, why, almighty as he is, should he have limited his power within any certain bounds? In favour of whom should he have renounced his privilege? Thy reason has in no other thing more of likelihood and foundation than in that wherein it persuades thee that there is a plurality of worlds:—

Terramque et solem, lunam, mare, estera quo rant,

Non esse unica, sed numro magis innumerali.

"That earth, sun, moon, sea, and the rest that are,

Not single, but innumerable were."

The most eminent minds of elder times believed it; and some of this age of ours, compelled by the appearances of human reason, do the same; forasmuch as in this fabric that we behold there is nothing single and one,

Cum in summ res nulla sit una,

Unica quo gignatur, et unica solaque crescat;

"Since nothing's single in this mighty place,

That can alone beget, alone increase;"

and that all the kinds are multiplied in some number; by which it seems not to be likely that God should have made this work only without a companion; and that the matter of this form should have been totally drained in this individual.

Quare etiam atque etiam tales fateare necesse est

Esse alios alibi congressus materiali;

Qualis hic est, avido complexu quem tenet ther.

"Wherefore 'tis necessary to confess

That there must elsewhere be the like congress

Of the like matter, which the airy space

Holds fast within its infinite embrace."

Especially if it be a living creature, which its motions render so credible that Plato affirms it, and that many of our people do either confirm, or dare not deny it; no more than that ancient opinion that the heavens, the stars, and other members of the world, are creatures composed of body and soul, mortal in respect of their composition, but immortal by the determination of the Creator. Now if there be many worlds, as Democritus, Epicurus, and almost all philosophy has believed, what do we know that the principles and rules of this of ours in like manner concern the rest? They may peradventure have another form and another polity. Epicurus supposes them either like or unlike. We see in this world an infinite difference and variety, only by distance of places; neither com, wine, nor any of our animals are to be seen in that new comer of the world discovered by our fathers; 'tis all there another thing; and in times past, do but consider in how many parts of the world they had no knowledge either of Bacchus or Ceres. If Pliny and Herodotus are to be believed, there are in certain places kinds of men very little resembling us, mongrel and ambiguous forms, betwixt the human and brutal natures; there are countries where men are bom without heads, having their mouth and eyes in their breast; where they are all hermaphrodites; where they go on all four; where they have but one eye in the forehead, and a head more like a dog than like ours; where they are half fish the lower part, and live in the water; where the women bear at five years old, and live but eight; where the head and the skin of the forehead is so hard that a sword will not touch it, but rebounds again; where men have no beards; nations that know not the use of fire; others that eject seed of a black colour. What shall we say of those that naturally change themselves into wolves, colts, and then into men again? And if it be true, as Plutarch says, that in some place of the Indies there are men without mouths, who nourish themselves with the smell of certain odours, how many of our descriptions are false? He is no longer risible, nor, perhaps, capable of reason and society. The disposition and cause of our internal composition would then for the most part be to no purpose, and of no use.

Moreover, how many things are there in our own knowledge that oppose those fine rules we have cut out for and prescribe to nature? And yet we must undertake to circumscribe thereto God himself! How many things do we call miraculous, and contrary to nature? This is done by every nation and by every man, according to the proportion of his ignorance. How many occult properties and quintessences do we daily discover? For, for us to go "according to nature," is no more but to go "according to our understanding," as far as that is able to follow, and as far as we are able to see into it; all beyond that is, forsooth, monstrous and irregular. Now, by this account, all things shall be monstrous to the wisest and most understanding men; for human reason has persuaded them that there was no manner of ground nor foundation, not so much as to be assured that snow is white, and Anaxagoras affirmed it to be black; if there be any thing, or if there be nothing; if there be knowledge or ignorance, which Metrodorus of Chios denied that man was able to determine; or whether we live, as Euripides doubts whether the life we live is life, or whether that we call death be not life, [—Greek—] and not without some appearance. For why do we derive the title of being from this instant, which is but a flash in the infinite course of an eternal night, and so short an interruption of our perpetual and natural condition, death possessing all the before and after this moment, and also a good part of the moment itself. Others swear there is no motion at all, as followers of Melissus, and that nothing stirs. For if there be but one, neither can that spherical motion be of any use to him, nor motion from one place to another, as Plato proves: "That there is neither generation nor corruption in nature." Protagoras says that there is nothing in nature but doubt; that a man may equally dispute of all things; and even of this, whether a man can equally dispute of all things; Nausiphanes, that of things which seem to be, nothing is more than it is not; that there is nothing certain but uncertainty; Parmenides, that of that which seems, there is no one thing in general; that there is but one thing; Zeno, that one same is not, and that there is nothing; if there were one thing, it would either be in another or in itself; if it be in another, they are two; if it be in itself, they are yet two; the comprehending, and the comprehended. According to these doctrines the nature of things is no other than a shadow, either false or vain.

This way of speaking in a Christian man has ever seemed to me very indiscreet and irreverent. "God cannot die; God cannot contradict himself; God cannot do this or that." I do not like to have the divine power so limited by the laws of men's mouths; and the idea which presents itself to us in those propositions ought to be more religiously and reverently expressed.

Our speaking has its failings and defects, as well as all the rest. Most of the occasions of disturbance in the world are grammatical ones; our suits only spring from disputes as to the interpretation of laws; and most wars proceed from the inability of ministers clearly to express the conventions and treaties of amity of princes. How many quarrels, and of how great importance, has the doubt of the meaning of this syllable, hoc,* created in the world? Let us take the clearest conclusion that logic itself

   * Montaigne here refers to the controversies between

   the Catholics and Protestants about transubstantiation.

presents us withal; if you say, "It is fine weather," and that you say true, it is then fine weather. Is not this a very certain form of speaking? And yet it will deceive us; that it will do so, let us follow the example: If you say, "I lie," if you say true, you do lie. The art, the reason, and force of the conclusion of this, are the same with the other, and yet we are gravelled. The Pyrrhonian philosophers, I see, cannot express their general conception in any kind of speaking; for they would require a new language on purpose; ours is all formed of affirmative propositions, which are totally antarctic to them; insomuch that when they say "I doubt," they are presently taken by the throat, to make them confess that at least they know and are assured that they do doubt. By which means they have been compelled to shelter themselves under this medical comparison, without which their humour would be inexplicable: when they pronounce, "I know not," or, "I doubt," they say that this proposition carries off itself with the rest, no more nor less than rhubarb, that drives out the ill humours, and carries itself off with them. This fancy will be more certainly understood by interrogation: "What do I know?" as I bear it with the emblem of a balance.

See what use they make of this irreverent way of speaking; in the present disputes about our religion, if you press its adversaries too hard, they will roundly tell you, "that it is not in the power of God to make it so, that his body should be in paradise and upon earth, and in several places at once." And see, too, what advantage the old scoffer made of this. "At least," says he, "it is no little consolation to man to see that God cannot do all things; for he cannot kill himself, though he would; which is the greatest privilege we have in our condition; he cannot make mortal immortal, nor revive the dead; nor make it so, that he who has lived has not; nor that he who has had honours has not had them; having no other right to the past than that of oblivion." And that the comparison of man to God may yet be made out by jocose examples: "He cannot order it so," says he, "that twice ten shall not be twenty." This is what he says, and what a Christian ought to take heed shall not escape his lips. Whereas, on the contrary, it seems as if men studied this foolish daring of language, to reduce God to their own measure:—

   Cras vel atr Nube polum, Pater, occupato,

Vel sole puro; non tamen irritum

Quodcumque retro est efficiet, neque

Diffinget infectumque reddet

Quod fugiens semel hora vexit.

   "To-morrow, let it shine or rain,

Yet cannot this the past make vain:

Nor uncreate and render void

That which was yesterday enjoyed."

When we say that the infinity of ages, as well past as to come, are but one instant with God; that his goodness, wisdom, and power are the same with his essence; our mouths speak it, but our understandings apprehend it not; and yet, such is our vain opinion of ourselves, that we must make the Divinity to pass through our sieve; and thence proceed all the dreams and errors with which the world abounds, whilst we reduce and weigh in our balance a thing so far above our poise. Mirum quo procdat improbitas cordis humani, parvulo aliquo intritata successu. "'Tis wonderful to what the wickedness of man's heart will proceed, if elevated with the least success." How magisterially and insolently does Epicurus reprove the Stoics, for maintaining that the truly good and happy being appertained only to God, and that the wise man had nothing but a shadow and resemblance of it! How temerariously have they bound God to destiny (a thing which, by my consent, none that bears the name of a Christian shall ever do again)! and Thales, Plato, and Pythagoras have enslaved him to necessity. This arrogance of attempting to discover God with our eyes has been the cause that an eminent person among us has attributed to the Divinity a corporal form; and is the reason of what happens to us every day, of attributing to God important events, by a particular assignment. Because they weigh with us, they conclude that they also weigh with him, and that he has a more intent and vigilant regard to them than to others of less moment to us or of ordinary course: Magna Dii curant, parva negligunt: "The gods are concerned at great matters, but slight the small." Listen to him; he will clear this to you by his reason: Nec in regnis quidem reges omnia minima curant: "Neither indeed do kings in their administration take notice of all the least concerns." As if to that King of kings it were more or less to subvert a kingdom, or to move the leaf of a tree; or as if his providence acted after another manner in inclining the event of a battle than in the leap of a flea. The hand of his government is laid upon every thing after the same manner, with the same power and order; our interest does nothing towards it; our inclinations and measures sway nothing with him. Deus ita artifex magnus in magnis, ut minor non sit in parvis: "God is so great an artificer in great things, that he is no less in the least" Our arrogancy sets this blasphemous comparison ever before us. Because our employments are a burden to us, Strato has courteously been pleased to exempt the gods from all offices, as their priests are; he makes nature produce and support all things; and with her weights and motions make up the several parts of the world, discharging human nature from the awe of divine judgments: Quod beatum terumque sit, id nec habere negotii quicquam, nec exhibere alteri: "What is blessed and eternal has neither any business itself nor gives any to another." Nature will that in like things there should be a like relation. The infinite number of mortals, therefore, concludes a like number of immortals; the infinite things that kill and destroy presupposes as many that preserve and profit. As the souls of the gods, without tongue, eye, or ear, do every one of them feel amongst themselves what the other feels, and judge our thoughts; so the souls of men, when at liberty and loosed from the body, either by sleep or some ecstacy, divine, foretell, and see things, which, whilst joined to the body, they could not see. "Men," says St. Paul, "professing themselves to be wise, they become fools; and change the glory of the uncorruptible God into an image made like corruptible man." Do but take notice of the juggling in the ancient deifications. After the great and stately pomp of the funeral, so soon as the fire began to mount to the top of the pyramid, and to catch hold of the couch where the body lay, they at the same time turned out an eagle, which flying upward, signified that the soul went into Paradise. We have a thousand medals, and particularly of the worthy Faustina, where this eagle is represented carrying these deified souls to heaven with their heels upwards. 'Tis pity that we should fool ourselves with our own fopperies and inventions,

  Quod finxere, timent,

"They fear their own inventions,"

like children who are frighted with the same face of their playfellow, that they themselves have smeared and smutted. Quasi quicquam infelicius sit homine, cui sua figmenta dominantur:

"As if any thing could be more unhappy than man, who is insulted over by his own imagination." 'Tis far from honouring him who made us, to honour him that we have made. Augustus had more temples than Jupiter, served with as much religion and belief of miracles. The Thracians, in return of the benefits they had received from Agesilaus, came to bring him word that they had canonized him: "Has your nation," said he to them, "the power to make gods of whom they please? Pray first deify some one amongst yourselves, and when I shall see what advantage he has by it, I will thank you for your offer." Man is certainly stark mad; he cannot make a worm, and yet he will be making gods by dozens. Hear Trismegistus in praise of our sufficiency: "Of all the wonderful things, it surmounts all wonder that man could find out the divine nature and make it." And take here the arguments of the school of philosophy itself:—

  Nosse cui divos et coli munina soli,

  Aut soli nescire, datum.

  "To whom to know the deities of heaven,

  Or know he knows them not, alone 'tis given."

"If there is a God, he is a living creature; if he be a living creature, he has sense; and if he has sense, he is subject to corruption. If he be without a body he is without a soul, and consequently without action; and if he has a body, it is perishable." Is not here a triumph? we are incapable of having made the world; there must then be some more excellent nature that has put a hand to the work. It were a foolish and ridiculous arrogance to esteem ourselves the most perfect thing of the universe. There must then be something that is better, and that must be God. When you see a stately and stupendous edifice, though you do not know who is the owner of it, you would yet conclude it was not built for rats. And this divine structure, that we behold of the celestial palace, have we not reason to believe that it is the residence of some possessor, who is much greater than we? Is not the most supreme always the most worthy? but we are in the lowest form. Nothing without a soul and without reason can produce a living creature capable of reason. The world produces us, the world then has soul and reason. Every part of us is less than we. We are part of the world, the world therefore is endued with wisdom and reason, and that more abundantly than we. 'Tis a fine thing to have a great government; the government of the world then appertains to some happy nature. The stars do us no harm; they are then full of goodness. We have need of nourishment; then so have the gods also, and feed upon the vapours of the earth. Worldly goods are not goods to God; therefore they are not goods to us; offending and being offended are equally testimonies of imbecility; 'tis therefore folly to fear God. God is good by his nature; man by his industry, which is more. The divine and human wisdom have no other distinction, but that the first is eternal; but duration is no accession to wisdom, therefore we are companions. We have life, reason, and liberty; we esteem goodness, charity, and justice; these qualities are then in him. In conclusion, building and destroying, the conditions of the Divinity, are forged by man, according as they relate to himself. What a pattern, and what a model! let us stretch, let us raise and swell human qualities as much as we please; puff up thyself, poor man, yet more and more, and more:—

Non, si tu ruperis, inquit.

"Not if thou burst," said he.

Profecto non Deum, quern cogitare non possunt, sed semetip pro illo cogitantes, non ilium, sed seipsos, non illi, sed sibi comparant? "Certainly they do not imagine God, whom they cannot imagine; but they imagine themselves in his stead; they do not compare him, but themselves, not to him, but to themselves." In natural things the effects do but half relate to their causes. What's this to the purpose? His condition is above the order of nature, too elevated, too remote, and too mighty, to permit itself to be bound and fettered by our conclusions. 'Tis not through ourselves that we arrive at that place; our ways lie too low. We are no nearer heaven on the top of Mount Cenis than at the bottom of the sea; take the distance with your astrolabe. They debase God even to the carnal knowledge of women, to so many times, and so many generations. Paulina, the wife of Satuminus, a matron of great reputation at Rome, thinking she lay with the god Serapis, found herself in the arms of an amoroso of hers, through the panderism of the priests of his temple. Varro, the most subtle and most learned of all the Latin authors, in his book of theology, writes, that the sexton of Hercules's temple, throwing dice with one hand for himself, and with the other for Hercules, played after that manner with him for a supper and a wench; if he won, at the expense of the offerings; if he lost, at his own. The sexton lost, and paid the supper and the wench. Her name was Laurentina, who saw by night this god in her arms, who moreover told her, that the first she met the next day, should give her a heavenly reward; which proved to be

Taruncius, a rich young man, who took her home to his house, and in time left her his inheritrix. She, in her turn, thinking to do a thing that would be pleasing to the god, left the people of Rome heirs to her; and therefore had divine honours attributed to her. As if it had not been sufficient that Plato was originally descended from the gods by a double line, and that he had Neptune for the common father of his race, it was certainly believed at Athens, that Aristo, having a mind to enjoy the fair Perictione, could not, and was warned by the god Apollo, in a dream, to leave her unpolluted and untouched, till she should first be brought to bed. These were the father and mother of Plato. How many ridiculous stories are there of like cuckoldings, committed by the gods against poor mortal men! And how many husbands injuriously scandaled in favour of the children! In the Mahometan religion there are Merlins enough found by the belief of the people; that is to say, children without fathers, spiritual, divinely conceived in the wombs of virgins, and carry names that signify so much in their language.

We are to observe that to every thing nothing is more dear and estimable than its being (the lion, the eagle the dolphin, prize nothing above their own kind); and that every thing assimilates the qualities of all other things to its own proper qualities, which we may indeed extend or contract, but that's all; for beyond that relation and principle our imagination cannot go, can guess at nothing else, nor possibly go out thence, nor stretch beyond it; whence spring these ancient conclusions: of all forms the most beautiful is that of man; therefore God must be of that form. No one can be happy without virtue, nor virtue be without reason, and reason cannot inhabit anywhere but in a human shape; God is therefore clothed in a human figure. Ita est informatum et anticipatum mentibus nostris, ut homini, quum de Deo cogitet, forma occurrat hu-mana. "It is so imprinted in our minds, and the fancy is so prepossessed with it, that when a man thinks of God, a human figure ever presents itself to the imagination." Therefore it was that Xenophanes pleasantly said, "That if beasts frame any gods to themselves, as 'tis likely they do, they make them certainly such as themselves are, and glorify themselves in it, as we do. For why may not a goose say thus; "All the parts of the universe I have an interest in; the earth serves me to walk upon; the sun to light me; the stars have their influence upon me; I have such an advantage by the winds and such by the waters; there is nothing that yon heavenly roof looks upon so favourably as me; I am the darling of nature! Is it not man that keeps, lodges, and serves me? 'Tis for me that he both sows and grinds; if he eats me he does the same by his fellow-men, and so do I the worms that kill and devour him." As much might be said by a crane, and with greater confidence, upon the account of the liberty of his flight, and the possession of that high and beautiful region. Tam blanda conciliatrix, et tam sui est lena ipsa natura. "So flattering and wheedling a bawd is nature to herself."

Now by the same consequence, the destinies are then for us; for us the world; it shines it thunders for us; creator and creatures, all are for us; 'tis the mark and point to which the universality of things aims. Look into the records that philosophy has kept for two thousand years and more, of the affairs of heaven; the gods all that while have neither acted nor spoken but for man. She does not allow them any other consultation or occupation. See them here against us in war:—

    Domitosque Hercule manu

Telluris juvenes, unde periculum

Fulgens contre mu it domus

Saturai veteris.

    "The brawny sons of earth, subdu'd by hand

Of Hercules on the Phlegran strand,

Where the rude shock did such an uproar make,

As made old Saturn's sparkling palace shake."

And here you shall see them participate of our troubles, to make a return for our having so often shared in theirs:—

    Neptunus muros, magnoque emota tridenti

Fundamenta quatit, totamque sedibus urbem

Emit: hie Juno Scas svissima portas Prima tenet.

    "Amidst that smother Neptune holds his place,

Below the walls' foundation drives his mace,

And heaves the city from its solid base.

See where in arms the cruel Juno stands,

Full in the Scan gate."

The Caunians, jealous of the authority of their own proper gods, armed themselves on the days of their devotion, and through the whole of their precincts ran cutting and slashing the air with their swords, by that means to drive away and banish all foreign gods out of their territory. Their powers are limited according that the plague, that the scurf, that the phthisic; one cures one sort of itch, another another: Adeo minimis etiam rebus prava religio inserit Deos? "At such a rate does false religion create gods for the most contemptible uses." This one makes grapes grow, that onions; this has the presidence over lechery, that over merchandise; for every sort of artisan a god; this has his province and reputation in the east; that his in the west:—

"Here lay her armour, here her chariot stood."

O sancte Apollo, qui umbilicum certum terrarum obtines!

"O sacred Phoebus, who with glorious ray,
From the earth's centre, dost thy light display."

Pallada Cecropid, Minola Creta Dianam,
Vulcanum tellus Hypsipylea colit,
Junonem Sparte, Pelopeladesque Mycen;
Pinigerum Fauni Mnalis ora caput;
Mars Latio venerandus.

"Th' Athenians Pallas, Cynthia Crete adore,
Vulcan is worshipped on the Lemnian shore.
Proud Juno's altars are by Spartans fed,
Th' Arcadians worship Faunus, and 'tis said
To Mars, by Italy, is homage paid."

to our necessity; this cures horses, that men,
  Hic illius arma, Hic currus fuit.
This has only one town or family in his possession; that lives alone; that in company, either voluntary or upon necessity:—

Junctaque sunt magno templa nepotis avo.

"And temples to the nephew joined are,

To those were reared to the great-grandfather."

In here are some so wretched and mean (for the number amounts to six and thirty thousand) that they must pack five or six together, to produce one ear of corn, and thence take their several names; three to a door—that of the plank, that of the hinge, and that of the threshold. Four to a child—protectors of his swathing-clouts, his drink, meat, and sucking. Some certain, some uncertain and doubtful, and some that are not yet entered Paradise:—

Quos, quoniam coli nondum dignamur honore,

Quas dedimus cert terras habitare sinanras:

"Whom, since we yet not worthy think of heaven,

We suffer to possess the earth we've given."

There are amongst them physicians, poets, and civilians. Some of a mean betwixt the divine and human nature; mediators betwixt God and us, adorned with a certain second and diminutive sort of adoration; infinite in titles and offices; some good; others ill; some old and decrepit, and some that are mortal. For Chrysippus was of opinion that in the last conflagration of the world all the gods were to die but Jupiter. Man makes a thousand pretty societies betwixt God and him; is he not his countryman?

Jovis incunabula Creten.

"Crete, the cradle of Jupiter."

And this is the excuse that, upon consideration of this subject, Scvola, a high priest, and Varro, a great theologian in their times, make us: "That it is necessary that the people should be ignorant of many things that are true, and believe many things that are false." Quum veritatem qua liberetur inquirat credatur ei expedire quod fallitur. "Seeing he inquires into the truth, by which he would be made free, 'tis fit he should be deceived." Human eyes cannot perceive things but by the forms they know; and we do not remember what a leap miserable Phton took for attempting to guide his father's horses with a mortal hand. The mind of man falls into as great a depth, and is after the same manner bruised and shattered by his own rashness. If you ask of philosophy of what matter the heavens and the sun are? what answer will she return, if not that it is iron, or, with Anaxagoras, stone, or some other matter that she makes use of? If a man inquire of Zeno what nature is? "A fire," says he, "an artisan, proper for generation, and regularly proceeding." Archimedes, master of that science which attributes to itself the precedency before all others for truth and certainty; "the sun," says he, "is a god of red-hot iron." Was not this a fine imagination, extracted from the inevitable necessity of geometrical demonstrations? Yet not so inevitable and useful but that Socrates thought it was enough to know so much of geometry only as to measure the land a man bought or sold; and that Polynus, who had been a great and famous doctor in it, despised it, as full of falsity and manifest vanity, after he had once tasted the delicate fruits of the lozely gardens of Epicurus. Socrates in Xenophon, concerning this affair, says of Anaxagoras, reputed by antiquity learned above all others in celestial and divine matters, "That he had cracked his brain, as all other men do who too immoderately search into knowledges which nothing belong to them:" when he made the sun to be a burning stone, he did not consider that a stone does not shine in the fire; and, which is worse, that it will there consume; and in making the sun and fire one, that fire does not turn the complexions black in shining upon them; that we are able to look fixedly upon fire; and that fire kills herbs and plants. 'Tis Socrates's opinion, and mine too, that the best judging of heaven is not to judge of it at all. Plato having occasion, in his Timous, to speak of the demons, "This undertaking," says he, "exceeds my ability." We are therefore to believe those ancients who said they were begotten by them; 'tis against all reason to refuse a man's faith to the children of the gods, though what they say should not be proved by any necessary or probable reasons; seeing they engage to speak of domestic and familiar things.

Let us see if we have a little more light in the knowledge of human and natural things. Is it not a ridiculous attempt for us to forge for those to whom, by our own confession, our knowledge is not able to attain, another body, and to lend a false form of our own invention; as is manifest in this motion of the planets; to which, seeing our wits cannot possibly arrive, nor conceive their natural conduct, we lend them material, heavy, and substantial springs of our own by which to move:—

Temo aureus, aurea summ

Curvatura rot, radiorum argenteus ordo.

"Gold was the axle, and the beam was gold;

The wheels with silver spokes on golden circles roll'd."

You would say that we had had coachmakers, carpenters, and painters, that went up on high to make engines of various motions, and to range the wheelwork and interfacings of the heavenly bodies of differing colours about the axis of necessity, according to Plato:—

Mundus domus est maxima rerum,

Quam quinque altiton fragmine zon

Cingunt, per quam limbus pictus bis sex signis

Stellimicantibus, altus in obliquo there, lun

Bigas acceptat.

"The world's a mansion that doth all things hold,

Which thundering zones, in number five, enfold,

Through which a girdle, painted with twelve signs,

And that with sparkling constellations, shines,

In heaven's arch marks the diurnal course

For the sun's chariot and his fiery horse."

These are all dreams and fanatic follies. Why will not nature please for once to lay open her bosom to us, and plainly discover to us the means and conduct of her movements, and prepare our eyes to see them? Good God, what abuse, what mistakes should we discover in our poor science! I am mistaken if that weak knowledge of ours holds any one thing as it really is, and I shall depart hence more ignorant of all other things than my own ignorance.

Have I not read in Plato this divine saying, that "nature is nothing but enigmatic poesy!" As if a man might perhaps see a veiled and shady picture, breaking out here and there with an infinite variety of false lights to puzzle our conjectures: Latent ista omnia crassis occullata et circumfusa tenebris; ut nulla acies humani ingenii tanta sit, qu penetrare in coelum, terram intrare, possit. "All those things lie concealed and involved in so dark an obscurity that no point of human wit can be so sharp as to pierce heaven or penetrate the earth." And certainly philosophy is no other than sophisticated poetry. Whence do the ancient writers extract their authorities but from the poets? and the first of them were poets themselves, and writ accordingly. Plato is but a poet unripped. Timon calls him, insultingly, "a monstrous forger of miracles." All superhuman sciences make use of the poetic style. Just as women make use of teeth of ivory where the natural are wanting, and instead of their true complexion make one of some artificial matter; as they stuff themselves out with cotton to appear plump, and in the sight of every one do paint, patch, and trick up themselves with a false and borrowed beauty; so does science (and even our law itself has, they say, legitimate fictions, whereon it builds the truth of its justice); she gives us in presupposition, and for current pay, things which she herself informs us were invented; for these epicycles, eccentrics, and concentrics, which astrology makes use of to carry on the motions of the stars, she gives us for the best she could invent upon that subject; as also, in all the rest, philosophy presents us not that which really is, or what she really believes, but what she has contrived with the greatest and most plausible likelihood of truth, and the quaintest invention. Plato, upon the discourse of the state of human bodies and those of beasts, says, "I should know that what I have said is truth, had I the confirmation of an oracle; but this I will affirm, that what I have said is the most likely to be true of any thing I could say."

'Tis not to heaven only that art sends her ropes, engines, and wheels; let us consider a little what she says of us ourselves, and of our contexture.

There is not more retrogradation, trepidation, accession, recession, and astonishment, in the stars and celestial bodies, than they have found out in this poor little human body. In earnest, they have good reason, upon that very account, to call it the little world, so many tools and parts have they employed to erect and build it. To assist the motions they see in man, and the various functions that we find in ourselves, in how many parts have they divided the soul, in how many places lodged it? in how many orders have they divided, and to how many stories have they raised this poor creature, man, besides those that are natural and to be perceived? And how many offices and vocations have they assigned him? They make it an imaginary public thing. 'Tis a subject that they hold and handle; and they have full power granted to them to rip, place, displace, piece, and stuff it, every one according to his own fancy, and yet they possess it not They cannot, not in reality only, but even in dreams, so govern it that there will not be some cadence or sound that will escape their architecture, as enormous as it is, and botched with a thousand false and fantastic patches. And it is not reason to excuse them; for though we are satisfied with painters when they paint heaven, earth, seas, mountains, and remote islands, that they give us some slight mark of them, and, as of things unknown, are content with a faint and obscure description; yet when they come and draw us after life, or any other creature which is known and familiar to us, we then require of them a perfect and exact representation of lineaments and colours, and despise them if they fail in it.

I am very well pleased with the Milesian girl, who observing the philosopher Thales to be always contemplating the celestial arch, and to have his eyes ever gazing upward, laid something in his way that he might stumble over, to put him in mind that it would be time to take up his thoughts about things that are in the clouds when he had provided for those that were under his feet. Doubtless she advised him well, rather to look to himself than to gaze at heaven; for, as Democritus says, by the mouth of Cicero,—

>   Quod est ante pedes, nemo spectat: coeli scrutantur plagas.

"No man regards what is under his feet;

They are always prying towards heaven."

But our condition will have it so, that the knowledge of what we have in hand is as remote from us, and as much above the clouds, as that of the stars. As Socrates says, in Plato, "That whoever meddles with philosophy may be reproached as Thales was by the woman, that he sees nothing of that which is before him. For every philosopher is ignorant of what his neighbour does; aye, and of what he does himself, and is ignorant of what they both are, whether beasts or men."

Those people, who find Sebond's arguments too weak, that are ignorant of nothing, that govern the world, that know all,—

Qu mare compescant caus; quid temperet annum;

Stell sponte su, jussve, vagentur et errent;

Quid premat obscurum lun, quid profrt orbem;

Quid velit et posait rerum concordia discors;

"What governs ocean's tides,

And through the various year the seasons guides;

Whether the stars by their own proper force,

Or foreign power, pursue their wand'ring course;

Why shadows darken the pale queen of night;

Whence she renews her orb and spreads her light;—

What nature's jarring sympathy can mean;"

have they not sometimes in their writings sounded the difficulties they have met with of knowing their own being? We see very well that the finger moves, that the foot moves, that some parts assume a voluntary motion of themselves without our consent, and that others work by our direction; that one sort of apprehension occasions blushing; another paleness; such an imagination works upon the spleen only, another upon the brain; one occasions laughter, another tears; another stupefies and astonishes all our senses, and arrests the motion of all our members; at one object the stomach will rise, at another a member that lies something lower; but how a spiritual impression should make such a breach into a massy and solid subject, and the nature of the connection and contexture of these admirable springs and movements, never yet man knew: Omnia incerta ratione, et in natur majestate abdita. "All uncertain in reason, and concealed in the majesty of nature," says Pliny. And St Augustin, Modus quo corporibus adhorent spiritus.... omnino minis est, nec comprehendi ab homine potest; et hoc ipse homo est, "The manner whereby souls adhere to bodies is altogether wonderful, and cannot be conceived by man, and yet this is man." And yet it is not so much as doubted; for the opinions of men are received according to the ancient belief, by authority and upon trust, as if it were religion and law. 'Tis received as gibberish which is commonly spoken; this truth, with all its clutter of arguments and proofs, is admitted as a firm and solid body, that is no more to be shaken, no more to be judged of; on the contrary, every one, according to the best of his talent, corroborates and fortifies this received belief with the utmost power of his reason, which is a supple utensil, pliable, and to be accommodated to any figure; and thus the world comes to be filled with lies and fopperies. The reason that men doubt of divers things is that they never examine common impressions; they do not dig to the root, where the faults and defects lie; they only debate upon the branches; they do not examine whether such and such a thing be true, but if it has been so and so understood; it is not inquired into whether Galen has said any thing to purpose, but whether he has said so or so. In truth it was very good reason that this curb to the liberty of our judgments and that tyranny over our opinions, should be extended to the schools and arts. The god of scholastic knowledge is Aristotle; 'tis irreligion to question any of his decrees, as it was those of Lucurgus at Sparta; his doctrine is a magisterial law, which, peradventure, is as false as another. I do not know why I should not as willingly embrace either the ideas of Plato, or the atoms of Epicurus, or the plenum or vacuum of Leucippus and Democritus, or the water of Thales, or the infinity of nature of Anaximander, or the air of Diogenes, or the numbers and symmetry of Pythagoras, or the infinity of Parmenides, or the One of Musus, or the water and fire of Apollodorus, or the similar parts of Anaxagoras, or the discord and friendship of Empedocles, or the fire of Heraclitus, or any other opinion of that infinite confusion of opinions and determinations, which this fine human reason produces by its certitude and clearsightedness in every thing it meddles withal, as I should the opinion of Aristotle upon this subject of the principles of natural things; which principles he builds of three pieces—matter, form, and privation. And what can be more vain than to make inanity itself the cause of the production of things? Privation is a negative; of what humour could he then make the cause and original of things that are? And yet that were not to be controverted but for the exercise of logic; there is nothing disputed therein to bring it into doubt, but to defend the author of the school from foreign objections; his authority is the non-ultra, beyond which it is not permitted to inquire.

It is very easy, upon approved foundations, to build whatever we please; for, according to the law and ordering of this beginning, the other parts of the structure are easily carried on without any failure. By this way we find our reason well-grounded, and discourse at a venture; for our masters prepossess and gain beforehand as much room in our belief as is necessary towards concluding afterwards what they please, as geometricians do by their granted demands, the consent and approbation we allow them giving them wherewith to draw us to the right and left, and to whirl us about at their pleasure. Whatever springs from these presuppositions is our master and our God; he will take the level of his foundations so ample and so easy that by them he may mount us up to the clouds, if he so please. In this practice and negotiation of science we have taken the saying of Pythagoras, "That every expert person ought to be believed in his own art" for current pay. The logician refers the signification of words to the grammarians; the rhetorician borrows the state of arguments from the logician; the poet his measure from the musician: the geometrician his proportions from the arithmetician, and the metaphysicians take physical conjectures for their foundations; for every science has its principle presupposed, by which human judgment is everywhere kept in check. If you come to rush against the bar where the principal error lies, they have presently this sentence in their mouths, "That there is no disputing with persons who deny principles." Now men can have no principles if not revealed to them by the divinity; of all the rest the beginning, the middle, and the end, is nothing but dream and vapour. To those that contend upon presupposition we must, on the contrary, presuppose to them the same axiom upon which the dispute is. For every human presupposition and declaration has as much authority one as another, if reason do not make the difference. Wherefore they are all to be put into the balance, and first the generals and those that tyrannize over us. The persuasion of certainty is a certain testimony of folly and extreme incertainty; and there are not a more foolish sort of men, nor that are less philosophers, than the Philodoxes of Plato; we must inquire whether fire be hot? whether snow be white? if there be any such things as hard or soft within our knowledge?

And as to those answers of which they make old stories, as he that doubted if there was any such thing as heat, whom they bid throw himself into the fire; and he that denied the coldness of ice, whom they bid to put ice into his bosom;—they are pitiful things, unworthy of the profession of philosophy. If they had let us alone in our natural being, to receive the appearance of things without us, according as they present themselves to us by our senses, and had permitted us to follow our own natural appetites, governed by the condition of our birth, they might then have reason to talk at that rate; but 'tis from them we have learned to make ourselves judges of the world; 'tis from them that we derive this fancy, "That human reason is controller-general of all that is without and within the roof of heaven; that comprehends every thing, that can do every thing; by the means of which every thing is known and understood." This answer would be good among the cannibals, who enjoy the happiness of a long, quiet, and peaceable life, without Aristotle's precepts, and without the knowledge of the name of physics; this answer would perhaps be of more value and greater force than all those they borrow from their reason and invention; of this all animals, and all where the power of the law of nature is yet pure and simple, would be as capable as we, but as for them they have renounced it. They need not tell us, "It is true, for you see and feel it to be so;" they must tell me whether I really feel what I think I do; and if I do feel it, they must then tell me why I feel it, and how, and what; let them tell me the name, original, the parts and junctures of heat and cold, the qualities of the agent and patient; or let them give up their profession, which is not to admit or approve of any thing but by the way of reason; that is their test in all sorts of essays; but, certainly, 'tis a test full of falsity, error, weakness, and defect.

Which way can we better prove it than by itself? If we are not to believe her when speaking of herself, she can hardly be thought fit to judge of foreign things; if she know any thing, it must at least be her own being and abode; she is in the soul, and either a part or an effect of it; for true and essential reason, from which we by a false colour borrow the name, is lodged in the bosom of the Almighty; there is her habitation and recess; 'tis thence that she imparts her rays, when God is pleased to impart any beam of it to mankind, as Balias issued from her father's head, to communicate herself to the world.

Now let us see what human reason tells us of herself and of the soul, not of the soul in general, of which almost all philosophy makes the celestial and first bodies participants; nor of that which Thales attributed to things which themselves are reputed inanimate, lead thereto by the consideration of the loadstone; but of that which appertains to us, and that we ought the best to know:—

Ignoratur enim, qu sit natura animai;

Nata sit; an, contra, nascentibus insinuetur;

Et simnl intereat nobiscum morte dirempta;

An tenebras Orci visat, vastasque lacunas,

An pecudes alias divinitns insinuet se.

"For none the nature of the soul doth know,

Whether that it be born with us, or no;

Or be infused into us at our birth,

And dies with us when we return to earth,

Or then descends to the black shades below,

Or into other animals does go."

Crates and Dicarchus were of opinion that there was no soul at all, but that the body thus stirs by a natural motion; Plato, that it was a substance moving of itself; Thales, a nature without repose; Aedepiades, an exercising of the senses; Hesiod and Anaximander, a thing composed of earth and water; Parmenides, of earth and fire; Empedocles, of blood:—

Sanguineam vomit ille animam;

"He vomits up his bloody soul."

Posidonius, Cleanthes, and Galen, that it was heat or a hot complexion—

Igneus est ollis vigor, et colestis origo;

"Their vigour of fire and of heavenly race."

Hippocrates, a spirit diffused all over the body; Varro, that it was an air received at the mouth, heated in the lungs, moistened in the heart, and diffused throughout the whole body; Zeno, the quintessence of the four elements; Heraclides Ponticus, that it was the light; Zenocrates and the Egyptians, a mobile number; the Chaldeans, a virtue without any determinate form:—

Habitum quemdam vitalem corporis esse,

Harmoniam Grci quam dicunt.

"A certain vital habit in man's frame,

Which harmony the Grecian sages name."

Let us not forget Aristotle, who held the soul to be that which naturally causes the body to move, which he calls entelechia, with as cold an invention as any of the rest; for he neither speaks of the essence, nor of the original, nor of the nature of the soul, but only takes notice of the effect Lactantius, Seneca, and most of the Dogmatists, have confessed that it was a thing they did not understand; after all this enumeration of opinions, Harum sententiarum quo vera sit, Deus aliquis viderit: "Of these opinions which is the true, let some god determine," says Cicero. "I know by myself," says St Bernard, "how incomprehensible God is, seeing I cannot comprehend the parts of my own being."

Heraclitus, who was of opinion that every being was full of souls and demons, did nevertheless maintain that no one could advance so far towards the knowledge of the soul as ever to arrive at it; so profound was the essence of it.

Neither is there less controversy and debate about seating of it. Hippocrates and Hierophilus place it in the ventricle of the brain; Democritus and Aristotle throughout the whole body;—

Ut bona spe valetudo cum dicitur esse

Corporis, et non est tamen hc pars ulla ralentis;

"As when the body's health they do it call,
When of a sound man, that's no part at all."

Epicurus in the stomach;

Hic exsultat enim pavor ac metus;
Hc loca circum Ltiti mulcent.

"For this the seat of horror is and fear,
And joys in turn do likewise triumph here."

The Stoics, about and within the heart; Erasistratus, adjoining the membrane of the epicranium; Empedocles, in the blood; as also Moses, which was the reason why he interdicted eating the blood of beasts, because the soul is there seated; Galen thought that every part of the body had its soul; Strato has placed it betwixt the eyebrows; Qu facie quidem sit animus, aut ubi habitet, ne quorendum quidem est: "What figure the soul is of, or what part it inhabits, is not to be inquired into," says Cicero. I very willingly deliver this author to you in his own words; for should I alter eloquence itself? Besides, it were but a poor prize to steal the matter of his inventions; they are neither very frequent, nor of any great weight, and sufficiently known. But the reason why Chrysippus argues it to be about the heart, as all the rest of that sect do, is not to be omitted; "It is," says he, "because when we would affirm any things we lay our hand upon our breasts; and when we would pronounce y, which signifies I, we let the lower jaw fall towards the stomach." This place ought not to be passed over without a remark upon the vanity of so great a man; for besides that these considerations are infinitely light in themselves, the last is only a proof to the Greeks that they have their souls lodged in that part. No human judgment is so sprightly and vigilant that it does not sometimes sleep. Why do we fear to say? The Stoics, the fathers of human prudence, think that the soul of a man, crushed under a ruin, long labours and strives to get out, like a mouse caught in a trap, before it can disengage itself from the burden. Some hold that the world was made to give bodies, by way of punishment, to the spirits fallen, by their own fault, from the purity wherein they had been created, the first creation having been incorporeal; and that, according as they are more or less depraved from their spirituality, so are they more or less jocundly or dully incorporated; and that thence proceeds all the variety of so much created matter. But the spirit that for his punishment was invested with the body of the sun must certainly have a very rare and particular measure of change.

The extremities of our perquisition do all fall into astonishment and blindness; as Plutarch says of the testimony of histories, that, according to charts and maps, the utmost bounds of known r countries are taken up with marshes, impenetrable forests, deserts, and uninhabitable places; this is the reason why the most gross and childish ravings were most found in those authors who treat of the most elevated subjects, and proceed the furthest in them, losing themselves in their own curiosity and presumption. The beginning and end of knowledge are equally foolish; observe to what a pitch Plato flies in his poetic clouds; do but take notice there of the gibberish of the gods; but what did he dream of when he defined a man to be "a two-legged animal without feathers: giving those who had a mind to deride him a pleasant occasion; for, having pulled a capon alive, they went about calling it the man of Plato."

And what did the Epicureans think of, out of what simplicity did they first imagine that their atoms that they said were bodies having some weight, and a natural motion downwards, had made the world; till they were put in mind, by their adversaries, that, according to this description, it was impossible they should unite and join to one another, their fall being so direct and perpendicular, and making so many parallel lines throughout? Wherefore there was a necessity that they should since add a fortuitous and sideways motion, and that they should moreover accoutre their atoms with hooked tails, by which they might unite and cling to one another. And even then do not those that attack them upon this second consideration put them hardly to it? "If the atoms have by chance formed so many sorts of figures, why did it never fall out that they made a house or a shoe? Why at the same rate should we not believe that an infinite number of Greek letters, strewed all over a certain place, might fall into the contexture of the Iliad?"—"Whatever is capable of reason," says Zeno, "is better than that which is not capable; there is nothing better than the world; the world is therefore capable of reason." Cotta, by this way of argumentation, makes the world a mathematician; 'and tis also made a musician and an organist by this other argumentation of Zeno: "The whole is more than a part; we are capable of wisdom, and are part of the world; therefore the world is wise." There are infinite like examples, not only of arguments that are false in themselves, but silly ones, that do not hold in themselves, and that accuse their authors not so much of ignorance as imprudence, in the reproaches the philosophers dash one another in the teeth withal, upon their dissensions in their sects and opinions.

Whoever should bundle up a lusty faggot of the fooleries of human wisdom would produce wonders. I willingly muster up these few for a pattern, by a certain meaning not less profitable to consider than the most sound and moderate instructions. Let us judge by these what opinion we are to have of man, of his sense and reason, when in these great persons that have raised human knowledge so high, so many gross mistakes and manifest errors are to be found.

For my part, I am apt to believe that they have treated of knowledge casually, and like a toy, with both hands; and have contended about reason as of a vain and frivolous instrument, setting on foot all sorts of fancies and inventions, sometimes more sinewy, and sometimes weaker. This same Plato, who defines man as if he were a cock, says elsewhere, after Socrates, "That he does not, in truth, know what man is, and that he is a member of the world the hardest to understand." By this variety and instability of opinions, they tacitly lead us, as it were by the hand, to this resolution of their irresolution. They profess not always to deliver their opinions barefaced and apparent to us; they have one while disguised them in the fabulous shadows of poetry, and at another in some other vizor; for our imperfection carries this also along with it, that crude meat is not always proper for our stomachs; we must dry, alter, and mix it; they do the same; they sometimes conceal their real opinions and judgments, and falsify them to accommodate themselves to the public use. They will not make an open profession of ignorance, and of the imbecility of human reason, that they may not fright children; but they sufficiently discover it to us under the appearance of a troubled and inconstant science.

I advised a person in Italy, who had a great mind to speak Italian, that provided he only had a desire to make himself understood, without being ambitious in any other respect to excel, that he should only make use of the first word that came to the tongue's end, whether Latin, French, Spanish, or Gascon, and that, by adding the Italian termination, he could not fail of hitting upon some idiom of the country, either Tuscan, Roman, Venetian, Piedmontese, or Neapolitan, and so fall in with some one of those many forms. I say the same of Philosophy; she has so many faces, so much variety, and has said so many things, that all our dreams and ravings are there to be found. Human fancy can conceive nothing good or bad that is not there: Nihil tam absurde did potest, quod non dicatur ab aliquo philosophorum. "Nothing can be said so absurd, that has not been said before by some of the philosophers." And I am the more willing to expose my whimsies to the public; forasmuch as, though they are spun out of myself, and without any pattern, I know they will be found related to some ancient humour, and some will not stick to say, "See whence he took it!" My manners are natural, I have not called in the assistance of any discipline to erect them; but, weak as they are, when it came into my head to lay them open to the world's view, and that to expose them to the light in a little more decent garb I went to adorn them with reasons and examples, it was a wonder to myself accidentally to find them conformable to so many philosophical discourses and examples. I never knew what regimen my life was of till it was near worn out and spent; a new figure—an unpremeditated and accidental philosopher.

But to return to the soul. Inasmuch as Plato has placed reason in the brain, anger in the heart, and concupiscence in the liver; 'tis likely that it was rather an interpretation of the movements of

the soul, than that he intended a division and separation of it, as of a body, into several members. And the most likely of their opinions is that 'tis always a soul, that by its faculty, reasons, remembers, comprehends, judges, desires, and exercises all its other operations by divers instruments of the body; as the pilot guides his ship according to his experience, one while straining or slacking the cordage, one while hoisting the mainyard, or removing the rudder, by one and the same power carrying on several effects; and that it is lodged in the brain; which appears in that the wounds and accidents that touch that part do immediately offend the faculties of the soul; and 'tis not incongruous that it should thence diffuse itself through the other parts of the body

> Medium non deserit unquam
>
> Coeli Phoebus iter; radiis tamen omnia lustrt.

> "Phoebus ne'er deviates from the zodiac's way;
>
> Yet all things doth illustrate with his ray."

As the sun sheds from heaven its light and influence, and fills the world with them:—

> Ctera pars animas, per totum dissita corpus,
>
> Paret, et ad numen mentis momenque movetur.

> "The other part o' th' soul diffus'd all o'er
>
> The body, does obey the reason's lore."

Some have said that there was a general soul, as it were a great body, whence all the particular souls were extracted, and thither again return, always restoring themselves to that universal matter:—

> Deum namque ire per omnes
>
> Terrasque, tractusque maris, columque profundum;
>
> Hinc pecudes, armenta, viros, genus omne ferarum,
>
> Quemque sibi tenues nascentem arcessere vitas:
>
> Scilicet hue reddi deinde, ac resoluta referri
>
> Omnia; nec morti esse locum:

"For God goes forth, and spreads throughout the whole

Heaven, earth, and sea, the universal soul;

Each at its birth, from him all beings share,

Both man and brute, the breath of vital air;

To him return, and, loos'd from earthly chain,

Fly whence they sprung, and rest in God again,

Spurn at the grave, and, fearless of decay,

Dwell in high heaven, and star th' ethereal way."

Others, that they only rejoined and reunited themselves to it; others, that they were produced from the divine substance; others, by the angels of fire and air; others, that they were from all antiquity; and some that they were created at the very point of time the bodies wanted them; others make them to descend from the orb of the moon, and return thither; the generality of the ancients believed that they were begotten from father to son, after a like manner, and produced with all other natural things; taking their argument from the likeness of children to their fathers;

    Instillata patris virtus tibi;

Fortes creantur fortibus, et bonis;

    "Thou hast thy father's virtues with his blood:

For still the brave spring from the brave and good;"

and that we see descend from fathers to their children not only bodily marks, but moreover a resemblance of humours, complexions, and inclinations of the soul:—

    Denique cur acris violentia triste leonum

Seminium sequitur? dolus vulpibus, et fuga, cervis

A patribus datur, et patrius pavor incitt artus?

Si non certa suo quia semine seminioque

Vis animi pariter crescit cum corpore toto.

"For why should rage from the fierce lion's seed,

Or from the subtle fox's craft, proceed;

Or why the tim'rous and flying hart

His fear and trembling to his race impart;

But that a certain force of mind does grow,

And still increases as the bodies do?"

That thereupon the divine justice is grounded, punishing in the children the faults of their fathers; forasmuch as the contagion of paternal vices is in some sort imprinted in the soul of children, and that the ill government of their will extends to them; moreover, that if souls had any other derivation than a natural consequence, and that they had been some other thins out of the body, they would retain some memory of their first being, the natural faculties that are proper to them of discoursing, reasoning, and remembering, being considered:—

Si in corpus nascentibus insinuatur,

Cur super anteactam tatem meminisse nequimus,

Nec vestigia gestarum rerum ulla tenemus?

"For at our birth if it infused be,

Why do we then retain no memory

Of our foregoing life, and why no more

Remember any thing we did before?"

for, to make the condition of our souls such as we would have it to be, we must suppose them all-knowing, even in their natural simplicity and purity; by these means they had been such, being free from the prison of the body, as well before they entered into it, as we hope they shall be after they are gone out of it; and from this knowledge it should follow that they should remember, being got in the body, as Plato said, "That what we learn is no other than a remembrance of what we knew before;" a thing which every one by experience may maintain to be false. Forasmuch, in the first place, as that we do not justly remember any thing but what we have been taught, and that if the memory did purely perform its office it would at least suggest to us something more than what we have learned. Secondly, that which she knew being in her purity, was a true knowledge, knowing things as they are by her divine intelligence; whereas here we make her receive falsehood and vice when we instruct her; wherein she cannot employ her reminiscence, that image and conception having never been planted in her. To say that the corporal prison does in such sort suffocate her natural faculties, that they are there utterly extinct, is first contrary to this other belief of acknowledging her power to be so great, and the operations of it that men sensibly perceive in this life so admirable, as to have thereby concluded that divinity and eternity past, and the immortality to come:—

Nam si tantopere est anirai mutata potestas,

Omnia ut actarum exciderit retinentia rerum,

Non, ut opinor, ea ab letho jam longior errat.

"For if the mind be changed to that degree

As of past things to lose all memory,

So great a change as that, I must confess,

Appears to me than death but little less."

Furthermore, 'tis here with us, and not elsewhere, that the force and effects of the soul ought to be considered; all the rest of her perfections are vain and useless to her; 'tis by her present condition that all her immortality is to be rewarded and paid, and of the life of man only that she is to render an account It had been injustice to have stripped her of her means and powers; to have disarmed her in order, in the time of her captivity and imprisonment in the flesh, of her weakness and infirmity in the time wherein she was forced and compelled, to pass an infinite and perpetual sentence and condemnation, and to insist upon the consideration of so short a time, peradventure but an hour or two, or at the most but a century, which has no more proportion with infinity than an instant; in this momentary interval to ordain and definitively to determine of her whole being; it were an unreasonable disproportion, too, to assign an eternal recompense in consequence of so short a life. Plato, to defend himself from this inconvenience, will have future payments limited to the term of a hundred years, relatively to human duration; and of us ourselves there are enough who have given them temporal limits. By this they judged that the generation of the soul followed the common condition of human things, as also her life, according to the opinion of Epicurus and Democritus, which has been the most received; in consequence of these fine appearances that they saw it bom, and that, according as the body grew more capable, they saw it increase in vigour as the other did; that its feebleness in infancy was very manifest, and in time its better strength and maturity, and after that its declension and old age, and at last its decrepitude:—

    Gigni pariter cum corpore, et una

    Crescere sentimus, pariterque senescere mentem.

    "Souls with the bodies to be born we may

    Discern, with them t' increase, with them decay."

They perceived it to be capable of divers passions, and agitated with divers painful motions, whence it fell into lassitude and uneasiness; capable of alteration and change, of cheerfulness, of stupidity and languor, and subject to diseases and injuries, as the stomach or the foot;

    Mentem sanari, corpus ut grum,

    Ceraimus, et flecti medicin posse videmus;

    "Sick minds, as well as bodies, we do see

    By Med'cine's virtue oft restored to be;"

dazzled and intoxicated with the fumes of wine, jostled from her seat by the vapours of a burning fever, laid asleep by the application of some medicaments, and roused by others,—

    Corpoream naturam animi esse necesse est,

    Corporeis quoniam telis ictuque laborat;

    "There must be of necessity, we find,

    A nature that's corporeal of the mind,

    Because we evidently see it smarts

    And wounded is with shafts the body darts;"

they saw it astonished and overthrown in all its faculties through the mere bite of a mad dog, and in that condition to have no stability of reason, no sufficiency, no virtue, no philosophical resolution, no resistance that could exempt it from the subjection of such accidents; the slaver of a contemptible cur shed upon the hand of Socrates, to shake all his wisdom and all his great and regulated imaginations, and so to annihilate them, ad that there remained no trace of his former knowledge,—

    Vis.... animal Conturbatur, et.... divisa seorsum

    Disjectatur, eodem illo distracta veneno;

    "The power of the soul's disturbed; and when

    That once is but sequestered from her, then

    By the same poison 'tis dispersed abroad;"

and this poison to find no more resistance in that great soul than in an infant of four years old; a poison sufficient to make all philosophy, if it were incarnate, become furious and mad; insomuch that Cato, who ever disdained death and fortune, could not endure the sight of a looking-glass, or of water, overwhelmed with horror and affright at the thought of falling, by the contagion of a mad dog, into the disease called by physicians hydrophobia:—

    Vis morbi distracta per artus

    Turbat agens animam, spumantes quore salso

    Ventorum ut validis fervescunt viribus und.

    "Throughout the limbs diffused, the fierce disease

    Disturbs the soul, as in the briny seas,

    The foaming waves to swell and boil we see,

    Stirred by the wind's impetuosity."

Now, as to this particular, philosophy has sufficiently armed man to encounter all other accidents either with patience, or, if the search of that costs too dear, by an infallible defeat, in totally depriving himself of all sentiment; but these are expedients that are only of use to a soul being itself, and in its full power, capable of reason and deliberation; but not at all proper for this inconvenience, where, in a philosopher, the soul becomes the soul of a madman, troubled, overturned, and lost; which many occasions may produce, as a too vehement agitation that any violent passion of the soul may beget in itself; or a wound in a certain part of the person, or vapours from the stomach, any of which may stupefy the understanding and turn the brain.

   Morbis in corporis avius errat

  Spe animus; dementit enim, deliraque fatur;

  Interdumque gravi lethargo fertur in altum

  ternumque soporem, oculis mi tuque cadenti:

  "For when the body's sick, and ill at ease,

  The mind doth often share in the disease;

  Wonders, grows wild, and raves, and sometimes by

  A heavy and a stupid lethargy,

  Is overcome and cast into a deep,

  A most profound and everlasting sleep."

The philosophers, methinks, have not much touched this string, no more than another of equal importance; they have this dilemma continually in their mouths, to console our mortal condition: "The soul is either mortal or immortal; if mortal, it will suffer no pain; if immortal, it will change for the better."—They never touch the other branch, "What if she change for the worse?" and leave to the poets the menaces of future torments. But thereby they make themselves a good game. These are two omissions that I often meet with in their discourses. I return to the first.

This soul loses the use of the sovereign stoical good, so constant and so firm. Our fine human wisdom must here yield, and give up her arms. As to the rest, they also considered, by the vanity of human reason, that the mixture and association of two so contrary things as the mortal and the immortal, was unimaginable:—

   Quippe etenim mortale terao jungere, et una

  Consentire putare, et fungi mutua posse,

  Desipere est. Quid enim diversius esse putandum est,

  Aut magis inter se disjunctum discrepitansque,

Quam, mortale quod est, immortali atque perenni

Junctum, in concilio, svas tolerare procellas?

"The mortal and th' eternal, then, to blend,

And think they can pursue one common end,

Is madness: for what things more diff'rent are.

Distinct in nature, and disposed to jar?

How can it then be thought that these should bear,

When thus conjoined, of harms an equal share?"

Moreover, they perceived the soul tending towards death as well as the body:—

Simul ovo fessa fatiscit:

"Fatigued together with the weight of years:"

which, according to Zeno, the image of sleep does sufficiently demonstrate to us; for he looks upon it "as a fainting and fall of the soul, as well as of the body:" Contrahi animum et quasi labi putat atque decidere: and, what they perceived in some, that the soul maintained its force and vigour to the last gasp of life, they attributed to the variety of diseases, as it is observable in men at the last extremity, that some retain one sense, and some another; one the hearing, and another the smell, without any manner of defect or alteration; and that there is not so universal a deprivation that some parts do not remain vigorous and entire:—

Non alio pacto, quam si, pes cum dolet gri,

In nullo caput interea sit forte dolore.

"So, often of the gout a man complains,

Whose head is, at the same time, free from pains."

The sight of our judgment is, to truth, the same that the owl's eyes are to the splendour of the sun, says Aristotle. By what can we better convince him, than by so gross blindness in so apparent a light? For the contrary opinion of the immortality of the soul, which, Cicero says, was first introduced, according to the testimony of books at least, by Pherecydes

Syrius, in the time of King Tullus (though some attribute it to Thales, and others to others), 'tis the part of human science that is treated of with the greatest doubt and

reservation. The most positive dogmatists are fain, in this point principally, to fly to the refuge of the Academy. No one doubts what Aristotle has established upon this subject, no more than all the ancients in general, who handle it with a wavering belief: Rem gratissimam promittentium magis quam probantium: "A thing more acceptable in the promisors than the provers." He conceals himself in clouds of words of difficult, unintelligible sense, and has left to those of his sect as great a dispute about his judgment as about the matter itself.

Two things rendered this opinion plausible to them; one, that, without the immortality of souls, there would be nothing whereon to ground the vain hopes of glory, which is a consideration of wonderful

repute in the world; the other, that it is a very profitable impression, as Plato says, that vices, when they escape the discovery and cognizance of human justice, are still within the reach of the divine, which will pursue them even after the death of the guilty. Man is excessively solicitous to prolong his being, and has to the utmost of his power provided for it; there are monuments for the conservation of the body, and glory to preserve the name. He has employed all his wit and opinion to the rebuilding of himself, impatient of his fortune, and to prop himself by his inventions. The soul, by reason of its anxiety and impotence, being unable to stand by itself, wanders up and down to seek out consolations, hopes, and foundations, and alien circumstances, to which she adheres and fixes; and how light or fantastic soever invention delivers them to her, relies more willingly, and with greater assurance, upon them than upon herself. But 'tis wonderful to observe how the most constant and obstinate maintainers of this just and clear persuasion of the immortality of the soul fall short, and how weak their arguments are, when they go about to prove it by human reason: Somnia sunt non docentis, sed optantis: "They are dreams, not of the teacher, but wisher," says one of the ancients. By which testimony man may know that he owes the truth he himself finds out to fortune and accident; since that even then, when it is fallen into his hand, he has not wherewith to hold and maintain it, and that his reason has not force to make use of it. All things produced by our own meditation and understanding, whether true or false, are subject to incertitude and controversy. 'Twas for the chastisement of our pride, and for the instruction of our miserable condition and incapacity, that God wrought the perplexity and confusion of the tower of Babel. Whatever we undertake without his assistance, whatever we see without the lamp of his grace, is but vanity and folly. We corrupt the very essence of truth, which is uniform and constant, by our weakness, when fortune puts it into our possession. What course soever man takes of himself, God still permits it to come to the same confusion, the image whereof he so lively represents to us in the just chastisement wherewith he crushed Nimrod's presumption, and frustrated the vain attempt of his proud structure; Perdam sapientiam sapientium, et prudentiam prudentium reprobabo. "I will destroy the wisdom of the wise, and will bring to nothing the understanding of the prudent." The diversity of idioms and tongues, with which he disturbed this work, what are they other than this infinite and perpetual alteration and discordance of opinions and reasons, which accompany and confound the vain building of human wisdom, and to very good effect too; for what would hold us, if we had but the least grain of knowledge? This saint has very much obliged me: Ipsa veritatis occultatio ant humili-tatis exercitatio est, aut elationis attritio "The very concealment of the truth is either an exercise of humility or a quelling of presumption." To what a pitch of presumption and insolence do we raise our blindness and folly!

But to return to my subject. It was truly very good reason that we should be beholden to God only, and to the favour of his grace, for the truth of so noble a belief, since from his sole bounty we receive the fruit of immortality, which consists in the enjoyment of eternal beatitude. Let us ingenuously confess that God alone has dictated it to us, and faith; for 'tis no lesson of nature and our own reason. And whoever will inquire into his own being and power, both within and without, without this divine privilege; whoever shall consider man impartially, and without flattery, will see in him no efficacy or faculty that relishes of any thing but death and earth. The more we give and confess to owe and render to God, we do it with the greater Christianity. That which this Stoic philosopher says he holds from the fortuitous consent of the popular voice; had it not been better that he had held it from God? Cum de animarum otemitate disserimus, non leve momentum apud nos habet consensus hominum aut timentium inferos, aut colentium. Utor hc public persuasione. "When we discourse of the immortality of souls, the consent of men that either fear or adore the infernal powers, is of no small advantage. I make use of this public persuasion." Now the weakness of human arguments upon this subject is particularly manifested by the fabulous circumstances they have superadded as consequences of this opinion, to find out of what condition this immortality of ours was. Let us omit the Stoics, (usuram nobis largiuntur tanquam cornicibus; diu mansuros aiunt animos; semper, negant. "They give us a long life, as also they do to crows; they say our soul shall continue long, but that it shall continue always they deny,") who give to souls a life after this, but finite. The most universal and received fancy, and that continues down to our times in various places, is that of which they make Pythagoras the author; not that he was the original inventor, but because it received a great deal of weight and repute by the authority of his approbation: "That souls, at their departure out of us, did nothing but shift from one body to another, from a lion to a horse, from a horse to a king, continually travelling at this rate from habitation to habitation;" and he himself said that he remembered he had been tha-lides, since that Euphorbus, afterwards Hermotimus, and, finally, from Pyrrhus was passed into Pythagoras; having a memory of himself of two hundred and six years. And some have added that these very souls sometimes mount up to heaven, and come down again:—

    O pater, aime aliquas ad colum hinc ire putandum est

> Sublimes animas, iterumque ad tarda reverti
>
> Corpora? Qu lucis miseris tam dira cupido?

> "O, father, is it then to be conceiv'd
>
> That any of these spirits, so sublime,
>
> Should hence to the celestial regions climb,
>
> And thence return to earth to reassume
>
> Their sluggish bodies rotting in a tomb?
>
> For wretched life whence does such fondness come?"

Origen makes them eternally to go and come from a better to a worse estate. The opinion that Varro mentions is that, after four hundred and forty years' revolution, they should be reunited to their first bodies; Chrysippus held that this would happen after a certain space of time unknown and unlimited. Plato, who professes to have embraced this belief from Pindar and the ancient poets, that we are to undergo infinite vicissitudes of mutation, for which the soul is prepared, having neither punishment nor reward in the other world but what is temporal, as its life here is but temporal, concludes that it has a singular knowledge of the affairs of heaven, of hell, of the world, through all which it has passed, repassed, and made stay in several voyages, are matters for her memory. Observe her progress elsewhere: "The soul that has lived well is reunited to the stars to which it is assigned; that which has lived ill removes into a woman, and if it do not there reform, is again removed into a beast of condition suitable to its vicious manners, and shall see no end of its punishments till it be returned to its natural constitution, and that it has, by the force of reason, purged itself from those gross, stupid, and elementary qualities it was polluted with." But I will not omit the objection the Epicureans make against this transmigration from one body to another; 'tis a pleasant one; they ask what expedient would be found out if the number of the dying should chance to be greater than that of those who are coming into the world. For the souls, turned out of their old habitation, would scuffle and crowd which should first get possession of their new lodging; and they further demand how they shall pass away their time, whilst waiting till new quarters are made ready for them? Or, on the contrary, if more animals should be born than die, the body, they say, would be but in an ill condition whilst waiting for a soul to be infused into it; and it would fall out that some bodies would die before they had been alive.

> Denique comrabia ad Veneris, partusque ferarum
>
> Esse animas prsto, deridiculum esse videtur;
>
> Et spectare immortales mortalia membra

Innumero numro, certareque prproperanter

Inter se, qu prima potissimaq insinueter.

"Absurd to think that whilst wild beasts beget,

Or bear their young, a thousand souls do wait,

Expect the falling body, fight and strive

Which first shall enter in and make it live."

Others have arrested the soul in the body of the deceased, with it to animate serpents, worms, and other beasts, which are said to be bred out of the corruption of our members, and even out of our ashes; others divide them into two parts, the one mortal, the other immortal; others make it corporeal, and nevertheless immortal. Some make it immortal, without

sense or knowledge. There are others, even among ourselves, who have believed that devils were made of the souls of the damned; as Plutarch thinks that gods were made of those that were saved; for there are few things which that author is so positive in as he is in this; maintaining elsewhere a doubtful and ambiguous way of expression. "We are told," says he, "and steadfastly should believe, that the souls of virtuous men, both according to nature and the divine justice, become saints, and from saints demigods, and from demigods, after they are perfectly, as in sacrifices of purgation, cleansed and purified, being delivered from all passibility and all mortality, they become, not by any civil decree, but in real truth, and according to all probability of reason, entire and perfect gods, in receiving a most happy and glorious end." But who desires to see him—him, who is yet the most sober and moderate of the whole gang of philosophers, lay about him with greater boldness, and relate his miracles upon this subject, I refer him to his treatise of the Moon, and of the Demon of Socrates, where he may, as evidently as in any other place whatever, satisfy himself that the mysteries of philosophy have many strange things in common with those of poetry; human understanding losing itself in attempting to sound and search all things to the bottom; even as we, tired and worn out with a long course of life, return to infancy and dotage. See here the fine and certain instructions which we extract from human knowledge concerning the soul.

Neither is there less temerity in what they teach us touching our corporal parts. Let us choose out one or two examples; for otherwise we should lose ourselves in this vast and troubled ocean of medical errors. Let us first know whether, at least, they agree about the matter whereof men produce one another; for as to their first production it is no wonder if, in a thing so high and so long since past, human understanding finds itself puzzled and perplexed. Archelaus, the physician, whose disciple and favourite Socrates was, according to Aristoxenus, said that both men and beasts were made of a lacteous slime, expressed by the heat of the earth; Pythagoras says that our seed is the foam or cream of our better blood; Plato, that it is the distillation of the marrow of the backbone; raising his argument from this, that that part is first sensible of being weary of the work; Alcmeon, that it is part of the substance of the brain, and that it is so, says he, is proved by the weakness of the eyes in those who are immoderate in that exercise; Democritus, that it is a substance extracted from the whole mass of the body; Epicurus, an extract from soul and body; Aristotle, an excrement drawn from the aliment of the blood, the last which is diffused over our members; others, that it is a blood concocted and digested by the heat of the genitals, which they judge, by reason that in excessive endeavours a man voids pure blood; wherein there seems to be more likelihood, could a man extract any appearance from so infinite a confusion. Now, to bring this seed to do its work, how many contrary opinions do they set on foot? Aristotle and Democritus are of opinion that women have no sperm, and that 'tis nothing but a sweat that they distil in the heat of pleasure and motion, and that contributes nothing at all to generation. Galen, on the contrary, and his followers, believe that without the concurrence of seeds there can be no generation. Here are the physicians, the philosophers, the lawyers, and divines, by the ears with our wives about the dispute, "For what term women carry their fruit?" and I, for my part, by the example of myself, stick with those that maintain a woman goes eleven months with child. The world is built upon this experience; there is no so commonplace a woman that cannot give her judgment in all these controversies; and yet we cannot agree.

Here is enough to verify that man is no better instructed in the knowledge of himself, in his corporal than in his spiritual part We have proposed himself to himself, and his reason to his reason, to see what she could say. I think I have sufficiently demonstrated how little she understands herself in herself; and who understands not himself in himself, in what can he? Quasi vero mensuram ullius rei possit agere, qui sui nesciat. "As if he could understand the measure of any other thing, that knows not his own." In earnest, Protagoras told us a pretty flam in making man the measure of all things, that never knew so much as his own; and if it be not he, his dignity will not permit that any other creature should have this advantage; now he being so contrary in himself, and one judgment so incessantly subverting another, this favourable proposition was but a mockery, which induced us necessarily to conclude the nullity of the compass and the compasser. When Thales reputes the knowledge of man very difficult for man to comprehend, he at the same time gives him to understand that all other knowledge is impossible.

You,* for whom I have taken the pains, contrary to my custom, to write so long a discourse, will not refuse to support your Sebond by the ordinary forms of arguing, wherewith you are every day instructed, and in this will exercise both your wit and learning; for this last fencing trick is never to be made use of but as an extreme remedy; 'tis a desperate thrust, wherein you are to quit your own arms to make your adversary abandon his; and a secret sleight, which must be very rarely, and then very reservedly, put in practice. 'Tis great temerity to lose yourself that you may destroy another; you must not die to be revenged, as Gobrias did; for, being closely grappled in combat with a lord of Persia, Darius coming in sword in hand, and fearing to strike lest he should kill Gobrias, he called out to him boldly to fall on,

* The author, as we have already mentioned, is addressing

Margaret de Valois.

though he should run them both through at once. I have known desperate weapons, and conditions of single combat, and wherein he that offered them put himself and his adversary upon terms of inevitable death to them both, censured for unjust. The Portuguese, in the Indian Sea, took certain Turks prisoners, who, impatient of their captivity, resolved, and it succeeded, by striking the nails of the ship one against another, and making a spark to fall into the barrels of powder that were set in the place where they were guarded, to blow up and reduce themselves, their masters, and the vessel to ashes. We here touch the out-plate and utmost limits of sciences, wherein the extremity is vicious, as in virtue. Keep yourselves in the common road; it is not good to be so subtle and cunning. Remember the Tuscan proverb:—

Chi troppo s'assottiglia, si scavezza.

"Who makes himself too wise, becomes a fool."

I advise you that, in all your opinions and discourses, as well as in your manners and all other things, you keep yourself moderate and temperate, and avoid novelty; I am an enemy to all extravagant ways. You, who by the authority of your grandeur, and yet more by the advantages which those qualities give you that are more your own, may with the twinkle of an eye command whom you please, ought to have given this charge to some one who made profession of letters, who might after a better manner have proved and illustrated these things to you. But here is as much as you will stand in need of.

Epicurus said of the laws, "That the worst were so necessary for us that without them men would devour one another." And Plato affirms, "That without laws we should live like beasts." Our wit is a wandering, dangerous, and temerarious utensil; it is hard to couple any order or measure to it; in those of our own time, who are endued with any rare excellence above others, or any extraordinary vivacity of understanding, we see them almost all lash out into licentiousness of opinions and manners; and 'tis almost a miracle to find one temperate and sociable. 'Tis all the reason in the world to limit human wit within the strictest limits imaginable; in study, as in all the rest, we ought to have its steps and advances numbered and fixed, and that the limits of its inquisition be bounded by art. It is curbed and fettered by religions, laws, customs, sciences, precepts, mortal and immortal penalties. And yet we see that it escapes from all these bonds by its volubility and dissolution; *tis a vain body which has nothing to lay hold on or to seize; a various and difform body, incapable of being either bound or held. In earnest, there are few souls so regular, firm, and well descended, as are to be trusted with their own conduct, and that can with moderation, and without temerity, sail in the liberty of their own judgments, beyond the common and received opinions; *tis more expedient to put them under pupilage. Wit is a dangerous weapon, even to the possessor, if he knows not how to use it discreetly; and there is not a beast to whom a headboard is more justly to be given, to keep his looks down and before his feet, and to hinder him from wandering here and there out of the tracks which custom and the laws have laid before him. And therefore it will be better for you to keep yourself in the beaten path, let it be what it will, than to fly out at a venture with this unbridled liberty. But if any of these new doctors will pretend to be ingenious in your presence, at the expense both of your soul and his own, to avoid this dangerous plague, which is every day laid in your way to infect you, this preservative, in the extremest necessity, will prevent the danger and hinder the contagion of this poison from offending either you or your company.

The liberty, then, and frolic forwardness of these ancient wits produced in philosophy and human sciences several sects of different opinions, every one undertaking to judge and make choice of what he would stick to and maintain. But now that men go all one way, Qui certis quibusdam destinatisque sententiis addicti et consecrati sunt, ut etiam, qu non probant, cogantur defendere, "Who are so tied and obliged to certain opinions that they are bound to defend even those they do not approve," and that we receive the arts by civil authority and decree, so that the schools have but one pattern, and a like circumscribed institution and discipline, we no more take notice what the coin weighs, and is really worth, but every one receives it according to the estimate that common approbation and use puts upon it; the alloy is not questioned, but how much it is current for. In like manner all things pass; we take physic as we do geometry; and tricks of hocus-pocus, enchantments, and love-spells, the correspondence of the souls of the dead, prognostications, domifications, and even this ridiculous pursuit of the philosophers' stone, all things pass for current pay, without any manner of scruple or contradiction. We need to know no more but that Mars' house is in the middle of the triangle of the hand, that of Venus in the thumb, and that of Mercury in the little finger; that when the table-line cuts the tubercle of the forefinger 'tis a sign of cruelty, that when it falls short of the middle finger, and that the natural median-line makes an angle with the vital in the same side, 'tis a sign of a miserable death; that if in a woman the natural line be open, and does not close the angle with the vital, this denotes that she shall not be very chaste. I leave you to judge whether a man qualified with such knowledge may not pass with reputation and esteem in all companies.

Theophrastus said that human knowledge, guided by the senses, might judge of the causes of things to a certain degree; but that being arrived to first and extreme causes, it must stop short and retire, by reason either of its own infirmity or the difficulty of things. 'Tis a moderate and gentle opinion, that our own understandings may conduct us to the knowledge of some things, and that it has certain measures of power, beyond which 'tis temerity to employ it; this opinion is plausible, and introduced by men of well composed minds, but 'tis hard to limit our wit, which is curious and greedy, and will no more stop at a thousand than at fifty paces; having experimentally found that, wherein one has failed, the other has hit, and that what was unknown to one age, the age following has explained; and that arts and sciences are not cast in a mould, but are formed and perfected by degrees, by often handling and polishing, as bears leisurely lick their cubs into form; what my force cannot discover, I do not yet desist to sound and to try; and by handling and kneading this new matter over and over again, by turning and heating it, I lay open to him that shall succeed me, a kind of facility to enjoy it more at his ease, and make it more maniable and supple for him,

   Ut hymettia sole

Cera remollescit, tractataque poll ice multas

Vertitur in facies, ipsoque fit utilis usu;

  "As wax doth softer in the sun become,

And, tempered 'twixt the finger and the thumb,

Will varions forms, and several shapes admit,

Till for the present use 'tis rendered fit;"

as much will the second do for the third; which is the cause that the difficulty ought not to make me despair, and my own incapacity as little; for 'tis nothing but my own.

Man is as capable of all things as of some; and if he confesses, as Theophrastus says, the ignorance of first causes, let him at once surrender all the rest of his knowledge; if he is defective in foundation, his reason is aground; disputation and inquiry have no other aim nor stop but principles; if this aim do not stop his career, he runs into an infinite irresolution. Non potest aliud alio magis minusve comprehendi, quoniam omnium rerum una est dejinitio comprehendendi:

"One thing can no more or less be comprehended than another, because the definition of comprehending all things is the same." Now 'tis very likely that, if the soul knew any thing, it would in the first place know itself; and if it knew any thing out of itself, it would be its own body and case, before any thing else. If we see the gods of physic to this very day debating about our anatomy,

   Mulciber in Trojam, pro Troj stabat Apollo;

"Vulcan against, for Troy Apollo stood;"

when are we to expect that they will be agreed? We are nearer neighbours to ourselves than whiteness to snow, or weight to stones. If man do not know himself, how should he know his force and functions? It is not, perhaps, that we have not some real knowledge in us; but 'tis by chance; forasmuch as errors are received into our soul by the same way, after the same manner, and by the same conduct, it has not wherewithal to distinguish them, nor wherewithal to choose the truth from falsehood.

The Academics admitted a certain partiality of judgment, and thought it too crude to say that it was not more likely to say that snow was white than black; and that we were no more assured of the motion of a stone, thrown by the hand, than of that of the eighth sphere. And to avoid this difficulty and strangeness, that can in truth hardly lodge in our imagination, though they concluded that we were in no sort capable of knowledge, and that truth is engulfed in so profound an abyss as is not to be penetrated by human sight; yet they acknowledged some things to be more likely than others, and received into their judgment this faculty, that they had a power to incline to one appearance more than another, they allowed him this propension, interdicting all resolution. The Pyrrhonian opinion is more bold, and also somewhat more likely; for this academic inclination, and this propension to one proposition rather than another, what is it other than a recognition of some more apparent truth in this than in that? If our understanding be capable of the form, lineaments, port, and face of truth, it might as well see it entire as by halves, springing and imperfect This appearance of likelihood, which makes them rather take the left hand than the right, augments it; multiply this ounce of verisimilitude that turns the scales to a hundred, to a thousand, ounces; it will happen in the end that the balance will itself end the controversy, and determine one choice, one entire truth. But why do they suffer themselves to incline to and be swayed by verisimilitude, if they know not the truth? How should they know the similitude of that whereof they do not know the essence? Either we can absolutely judge, or absolutely we cannot If our intellectual and sensible faculties are without foot or foundation, if they only pull and drive, 'tis to no purpose that we suffer our judgments to be carried away with any part of their operation, what appearance soever they may seem to present us; and the surest and most happy seat of our understanding would be that where it kept itself temperate, upright, and inflexible, without tottering, or without agitation: Inter visa, vera aut falsa, ad animi assensum, nihil interest: "Amongst things that seem, whether true or false, it signifies nothing to the assent of the mind." That things do not lodge in us in their form and essence, and do not there make their entry by their own force and authority, we sufficiently see; because, if it were so, we should receive them after the same manner; wine would have the same relish with the sick as with the healthful; he who has his finger chapt or benumbed would find the same hardness in wood or iron that he handles that another does; foreign subjects then surrender themselves to our mercy, and are seated in us as we please. Now if on our part we received any thing without alteration, if human grasp were capable and strong enough to seize on truth by our own means, these means being common to all men, this truth would be conveyed from hand to hand, from one to another; and at least there would be some one thing to be found in the world, amongst so many as there are, that would be believed by men with an universal consent; but this, that there is no one proposition that is not debated and controverted amongst us, or that may not be, makes it very manifest that our natural judgment does not very clearly discern what it embraces; for my judgment cannot make my companions approve of what it approves; which is a sign that I seized it by some other means than by a natural power that is in me and in all other men.

Let us lay aside this infinite confusion of opinions, which we see even amongst the philosophers themselves, and this perpetual and universal dispute about the knowledge of things; for this is truly presupposed, that men, I mean the most knowing, the best bom, and of the best parts, are not agreed about any one thing, not that heaven is over our heads; for they that doubt of every thing, do also doubt of that; and they who deny that we are able to comprehend any thing, say that we have not comprehended that the heaven is over our heads, and these two opinions are, without comparison, the stronger in number.

Besides this infinite diversity and division, through the trouble that our judgment gives ourselves, and the incertainty that every one is sensible of in himself, 'tis easy to perceive that its seat is very unstable and insecure. How variously do we judge of things?—How often do we alter our opinions? What I hold and believe to-day I hold and believe with my whole belief; all my instruments and engines seize and take hold of this opinion, and become responsible to me for it, at least as much as in them lies; I could not embrace nor conserve any truth with greater confidence and assurance than I do this; I am wholly and entirely possessed with it; but has it not befallen me, not only once, but a hundred, a thousand times, every day, to have embraced some other thing with all the same instruments, and in the same condition, which I have since judged to be false? A man must at least become wise at his own expense; if I have often found myself betrayed under this colour; if my touch proves commonly false, and my balance unequal and unjust, what assurance can I now have more than at other times? Is it not stupidity and madness to suffer myself to be so often deceived by my guide? Nevertheless, let fortune remove and shift us five hundred times from place to place, let her do nothing but incessantly empty and fill into our belief, as into a vessel, other and other opinions; yet still the present and the last is the certain and infallible one; for this we must abandon goods, honour, life, health, and all.

    Posterior.... res ilia reperta

Perdit, et immutat sensus ad pristina qnqne.

"The last things we find out are always best,

And make us to disrelish all the rest."

Whatever is preached to us, and whatever we learn, we should still remember that it is man that gives and man that receives; 'tis a mortal hand that presents it to us; 'tis a mortal hand that accepts it The things that come to us from heaven have the sole right and authority of persuasion, the sole mark of truth; which also we do not see with our own eyes, nor receive by our own means; that great and sacred image could not abide in so wretched a habitation if God for this end did not prepare it, if God did not by his particular and supernatural grace and favour fortify and reform it. At least our frail and defective condition ought to make us behave ourselves with more reservedness and moderation in our innovations and changes; we ought to remember that, whatever we receive into the understanding, we often receive things that are false, and that it is by the same instruments that so often give themselves the lie and are so often deceived.

Now it is no wonder they should so often contradict themselves, being so easy to be turned and swayed by very light occurrences. It is certain that our apprehensions, our judgment, and the faculties of the soul in general, suffer according to the movements and alterations of the body, which alterations are continual. Are not our minds more sprightly, ou memories more prompt and quick, and our thoughts morc livcly, in health than in sickness? Do not joy and gayety make us receive subjects that present themselves to our souls quite otherwise than care and melancholy? Do you believe that Catullus's verses, or those of Sappho, please an old doting miser as they do a vigorous, amorous young man? Cleomenes, the son of Anexandridas, being sick, his friends reproached him that he had humours and whimsies that were new and unaccustomed; "I believe it," said he; "neither am I the same man now as when I am in health; being now another person, my opinions and fancies are also other than they were before." In our courts of justice this word is much in use, which is spoken of criminals when they find the judges in a good humour, gentle, and mild, Gaudeat de bon fortun ; "Let him rejoice in his good fortune;" for it is most certain that men's judgments are sometimes more prone to condemnation, more sharp and severe, and at others more facile, easy, and inclined to excuse; he that carries with him from his house the pain of the gout, jealousy, or theft by his man, having his whole soul possessed with anger, it is not to be doubted but that his judgment will lean this way. That venerable senate of the Areopagites used to hear and determine by night, for fear lest the sight of the parties might corrupt their justice. The very air itself, and the serenity of heaven, will cause some mutation in us, according to these verses in Cicero:—

Tales sunt hominnm mentes, quali pater ipse

Jupiter auctifer lustravit lampade terras.

"Men's minds are influenc'd by th' external air,

Dark or serene, as days are foul or fair."

'Tis not only fevers, debauches, and great accidents, that overthrow our judgments,—the least things in the world will do it; and we are not to doubt, though we may not be sensible of it, that if a continued fever can overwhelm the soul, a tertian will in some proportionate measure alter it; if an apoplexy can stupefy and totally extinguish the sight of our understanding, we are not to doubt but that a great cold will dazzle it; and consequently there is hardly one single hour in a man's whole life wherein our judgment is in its due place and right condition, our bodies being subject to so many continual mutations, and stuffed with so many several sorts of springs, that I believe the physicians, that it is hard but that there must be always some one or other out of order.

As to what remains, this malady does not very easily discover itself, unless it be extreme and past remedy; forasmuch as reason goes always lame, halting, and that too as well with falsehood as with truth; and therefore 'tis hard to discover her deviations and mistakes. I always call that appearance of meditation which every one forges in himself reason; this reason, of the condition of which there may be a hundred contrary ones about one and the same subject, is an instrument of lead and of wax, ductile, pliable, and accommodate to all sorts of biases, and to all measures; so that nothing remains but the art and skill how to turn and mould it. How uprightly soever a judge may mean, if he does not look well to himself, which few care to do, his inclination to friendship, to relationship, to beauty or revenge, and not only things of that weight, but even the fortuitous instinct that makes us favour one thing more than another, and that, without reason's permission, puts the choice upon us in two equal subjects, or some shadow of like vanity, may insensibly insinuate into his judgment the recommendation or disfavour of a cause, and make the balance dip.

I, that watch myself as narrowly as I can, and that have my eyes continually bent upon myself, like one that has no great business to do elsewhere,

> Quis sub Arcto Rex gelid metuatur or,
>
> Quid Tyridatem terreat, unice Securus,

> "I care not whom the northern clime reveres,
>
> Or what's the king that Tyridates fears,"

dare hardly tell the vanity and weakness I find in myself My foot is so unstable and unsteady, I find myself so apt to totter and reel, and my sight so disordered, that, fasting, I am quite another man than when full; if health and a fair day smile upon me, I am a very affable, good-natured man; if a corn trouble my toe, I am sullen, out of humour, and not to be seen. The same pace of a horse seems to me one while hard, and another easy; and the same way one while shorter, and another longer; and the same form one while more, another less agreeable: I am one while for doing every thing, and another for doing nothing at all; and what pleases me now would be a trouble to me at another time. I have a thousand senseless and casual actions within myself; either I am possessed by melancholy or swayed by choler; now by its own private authority sadness predominates in me, and by and by, I am as merry as a cricket. When I take a book in hand I have then discovered admirable graces in such and such passages, and such as have struck my soul; let me light upon them at another time, I may turn and toss, tumble and rattle the leaves to no purpose; 'tis then to me an inform and undiscovered mass. Even in my own writings I do not always find the air of my first fancy; I know not what I would have said, and am often put to it to correct and pump for a new sense, because I have lost the first that was better. I do nothing but go and come; my judgment does not always advance—it floats and roams:—

Velut minuta magno

Deprensa navis in mari vesaniente vento.

"Like a small bark that's tost upon the main.

When winds tempestuous heave the liquid plain."

Very often, as I am apt to do, having for exercise taken to maintain an opinion contrary to my own, my mind, bending and applying itself that way, does so engage me that way that I no more discern the reason of my former belief, and forsake it I am, as it were, misled by the side to which I incline, be it what it will, and carried away by my own weight. Every one almost would say the same of himself, if he considered himself as I do. Preachers very well know that the emotions which steal upon them in speaking animate them towards belief; and that in passion we are more warm in the defence of our proposition, take ourselves a deeper impression of it, and embrace it with greater vehemence and approbation than we do in our colder and more temperate state. You only give your counsel a simple brief of your cause; he returns you a dubious and uncertain answer, by which you find him indifferent which side he takes. Have you feed him well that he may relish it the better, does he begin to be really concerned, and do you find him interested and zealous in your quarrel? his reason and learning will by degrees grow hot in your cause; behold an apparent and undoubted truth presents itself to his understanding; he discovers a new light in your business, and does in good earnest believe and persuade himself that it is so. Nay, I do not know whether the ardour that springs from spite and obstinacy, against the power and violence of the magistrate and danger, or the interest of reputation, may not have made some men, even at the stake, maintain the opinion for which, at liberty, and amongst friends, they would not have burned a finger. The shocks and jostles that the soul receives from the body's passions can do much in it, but its own can do a great deal more; to which it is so subjected that perhaps it may be made good that it has no other pace and motion but from the breath of those winds, without the agitation of which it would be becalmed and without action, like a ship in the middle of the sea, to which the winds hare denied their assistance. And whoever should maintain this, siding with the Peripatetics, would do us no great wrong, seeing it is very well known that the greatest and most noble actions of the soul proceed from, and stand in need of, this impulse of the passions. Valour, they say, cannot be perfect without the assistance of anger; Semper Ajax fortis, fortissimus tamen in furore; "Ajax was always brave, but most when in a fury:" neither do we encounter the wicked and the enemy vigorously enough if we be not angry; nay, the advocate, it is said, is to inspire the judges with indignation, to obtain justice.

Irregular desires moved Themistocles, and Demosthenes, and have pushed on the philosophers to watching, fasting, and pilgrimages; and lead us to honour, learning, and health, which are all very useful ends. And this meanness of soul, in suffering anxiety and trouble, serves to breed remorse and repentance in the conscience, and to make us sensible of the scourge of God, and politic correction for the chastisement of our offences; compassion is a spur to clemency; and the prudence of preserving and governing ourselves is roused by our fear; and how many brave actions by ambition! how many by presumption! In short, there is no brave and spiritual virtue without some irregular agitation. May not this be one of the reasons that moved the Epicureans to discharge God from all care and solicitude of our affairs; because even the effects of his goodness could not be exercised in our behalf without disturbing its repose, by the means of passions which are so many spurs and instruments pricking on the soul to virtuous actions; or have they thought otherwise, and taken them for tempests, that shamefully hurry the soul from her tranquillity? Ut maris tranquillitas intettigitur, null, ne minima quidem, aura fluctus commovente: Sic animi quietus et placatus status cemitur, quum perturbatis nulla est, qua moveri queat.. "As it is understood to be a calm sea when there is not the least breath of air stirring; so the state of the soul is discerned to be quiet and appeased when there is no perturbation to move it."

What varieties of sense and reason, what contrariety of imaginations does the diversity of our passions inspire us with! What assurance then can we take of a thing so mobile and unstable, subject by its condition to the dominion of trouble, and never going other than a forced and borrowed pace? If our judgment be in the power even of sickness and perturbation; if it be from folly and rashness that it is to receive the impression of things, what security can we expect from it?

Is it not a great boldness in philosophy to believe that men perform the greatest actions, and nearest approaching the Divinity, when they are furious, mad, and beside themselves? We better ourselves by the privation of our reason, and drilling it. The two natural ways to enter into the cabinet of the gods, and there to foresee the course of destiny, are fury and sleep.

This is pleasant to consider; by the dislocation that passions cause in our reason, we become virtuous; by its extirpation, occasioned by madness or the image of death, we become diviners and prophets. I was never so willing to believe philosophy in any thing as this. 'Tis a pure enthusiasm wherewith sacred truth has inspired the spirit of philosophy, which makes it confess, contrary to its own proposition, that the most calm, composed, and healthful estate ef the soul that philosophy can seat it in is not its best condition; our waking is more a sleep than sleep itself, our wisdom less wise than folly; our dreams are worth more than our meditation; and the worst place we can take is in ourselves. But does not philosophy think that we are wise enough to consider that the voice that the spirit utters, when dismissed from man, so clear-sighted, so great, and so perfect, and whilst it is in man so terrestrial, ignorant, and dark, is a voice proceeding from the spirit of dark, terrestrial, and ignorant man, and for this reason a voice not to be trusted and believed?

I, being of a soft and heavy complexion, have no great experience of these vehement agitations, the most of which surprise the soul on a sudden, without giving it leisure to recollect itself. But the passion that is said to be produced by idleness in the hearts of young men, though it proceed leisurely, and with a measured progress, does evidently manifest, to those who have tried to oppose its power, the violence our judgment suffers in this alteration and conversion. I have formerly attempted to withstand and repel it; for I am so far from being one of those that invite vices, that I do not so much as follow them, if they do not haul me along; I perceived it to spring, grow, and increase, in spite of my resistance; and at last, living and seeing as I was, wholly to seize and possess me. So that, as if rousing from drunkenness, the images of things began to appear to me quite other than they used to be; I evidently saw the advantages of the object I desired, grow, and increase, and expand by the influence of my imagination, and the difficulties of my attempt to grow more easy and smooth; and both my reason and conscience to be laid aside; but this fire being evaporated in an instant, as from a flash of lightning, I was aware that my soul resumed another kind of sight, another state, and another judgment; the difficulties of retreat appeared great and invincible, and the same things had quite another taste and aspect than the heat of desire had presented them to me; which of the two most truly? Pyrrho knows nothing about it. We are never without sickness. Agues have their hot and cold fits; from the effects of an ardent passion we fall again to shivering; as much as I had advanced, so much I retired:—

Qualis ubi alterno procurrens gurgite pontus,

Nunc ruit ad terras, scopulosque superjacit undam

Spumeus, extremamque sinu perfundit arenam;

Nunc rapidus retro, atque stu revoluta resorbens

Saxa, fugit, littusque vado labente relihquit.

"So swelling surges, with a thundering roar,

Driv'n on each others' backs, insult the shore,

Bound o'er the rocks, encroach upon the land,

And far upon the beach heave up the sand;

Then backward rapidly they take their way,

Repulsed from upper ground, and seek the sea."

Now, from the knowledge of this volubility of mine, I have accidentally begot in myself a certain constancy of opinions, and have not much altered those that were first and natural in me; for what appearance soever there may be in novelty, I do not easily change, for fear of losing by the bargain; and, as I am not capable of choosing, I take other men's choice, and keep myself in the station wherein God has placed me; I could not otherwise keep myself from perpetual rolling. Thus have I, by the grace of God, preserved myself entire, without anxiety or trouble of conscience, in the ancient faith of our religion, amidst so many sects and divisions as our age has produced. The writings of the ancients, the best authors I mean, being full and solid, tempt and carry me which way almost they will; he that I am reading seems always to have the most force; and I find that every one in his turn is in the right, though they contradict one another. The facility that good wits have of rendering every thing likely they would recommend, and that nothing is so strange to which they do not undertake to give colour enough to deceive such simplicity as mine, this evidently shows the weakness of their testimony. The heavens and the stars have been three thousand years in motion; all the world were of that belief till Cleanthes the Samian, or, according to Theophrastus, Nicetas of Syracuse, took it into his head to maintain that it was the earth that moved, turning about its axis by the oblique circle of the zodiac. And Copernicus has in our times so grounded this doctrine that it very regularly serves to all astrological consequences; what use can we make of this, if not that we ought not much to care which is the true opinion? And who knows but that a third, a thousand years hence, may over throw the two former.

    Sic volvenda tas commutt tempora rerum:

Quod fuit in pretio, fit nullo denique honore;

Porro aliud succedit, et e contemptibus exit,

Inque dies magis appetitur, floretque repertum

Laudibus, et miro est mortales inter honore.

    "Thus ev'ry thing is changed in course of time,

What now is valued passes soon its prime;

To which some other thing, despised before,

Succeeds, and grows in vogue still more and more;

And once received, too faint all praises seem,

So highly it is rais'd in men's esteem."

So that when any new doctrine presents itself to us, we have great reason to mistrust, and to consider that, before that was set on foot, the contrary had been generally received; and that, as that has been overthrown by this, a third invention, in time to come, may start up which may damn the second. Before the principles that Aristotle introduced were in reputation, other principles contented human reason, as these satisfy us now. What patent have these people, what particular privilege, that the career of our invention must be stopped by them, and that the possession of our whole future belief should belong to them? They are no more exempt from being thrust out of doors than their predecessors were. When any one presses me with a new argument, I ought to believe that what I cannot answer another can; for to believe all likelihoods that a man cannot confute is great simplicity; it would by that means come to pass that all the vulgar (and we are all of the vulgar) would have their belief as tumable as a weathercock; for their souls, being so easy to be imposed upon, and without any resistance, must of force incessantly receive other and other impressions, the last still effacing all footsteps of that which went before. He that finds himself weak ought to answer, according to practice, that he will speak with his counsel, or refer himself to the wiser, from whom he received his instruction. How long is it that physic has been practised in the world? 'Tis said that a new comer, called Paracelsus, changes and overthrows the whole order of ancient rules, and maintains that, till now, it has been of no other use but to kill men. I believe he will easily make this good, but I do not think it were wisdom to venture my life in making trial of his own experience. We are not to believe every one, says the precept, because every one can say all things. A man of this profession of novelties and physical reformations not long since told me that all the ancients were notoriously mistaken in the nature and motions of the winds, which he would evidently demonstrate to me if I would give him the hearing. After I had with some patience heard his arguments, which were all full of likelihood of truth: "What, then," said I, "did those that sailed according to Theophrastus make way westward, when they had the prow towards the east? did they go sideward or backward?" "That's fortune," answered he, "but so it is that they were mistaken." I replied that I had rather follow effects than reason. Now these are things that often interfere with one another, and I have been told that in geometry (which pretends to have gained the highest point of certainty of all science) there are inevitable demonstrations found which subvert the truth of all experience; as Jacques Pelletier told me, at my own house, that he had found out two lines stretching themselves one towards the other to meet, which nevertheless he affirmed, though extended to infinity, could never arrive to touch one another. And the Pyrrhonians make no other use of their arguments and their reason than to ruin the appearance of experience; and 'tis a wonder how far the suppleness of our reason has followed them in this design of controverting the evidence of effects; for they affirm that we do not move, that we do not speak, and that there is neither weight nor heat, with the same force of argument that we affirm the most likely things. Ptolemy, who was a great man, had established the bounds of this world of ours; all the ancient philosophers thought they had the measure of it, excepting some remote isles that might escape their knowledge; it had been Pyrrhonism, a thousand years ago, to doubt the science of cosmography, and the opinions that every one had received from it; it was heresy to admit the antipodes; and behold, in this age of ours, there is an infinite extent of terra firma discovered, not an island or single country, but a division of the world, nearly equal in greatness to that we knew before. The geographers of our time stick not to assure us that now all is found; all is seen:—

Nam quod adest prosto, placet, et pollere videtur;

"What's present pleases, and appears the best;"

but it remains to be seen whether, as Ptolemy was therein formerly deceived upon the foundation of his reason, it were not very foolish to trust now in what these people say? And whether it is not more likely that this great body, which we call the world, is not quite another thing than what we imagine.

Plato says that it changes countenance in all respects; that the heavens, the stars, and the sun, have all of them sometimes motions retrograde to what we see, changing east into west The Egyptian priests told Herodotus that from the time of their first king, which was eleven thousand and odd years since (and they showed him the effigies of all their kings in statues taken from the life), the sun had four times altered his course; that the sea and the earth did alternately change into one another; that the beginning of the world is undetermined; Aristotle and Cicero both say the same; and some amongst us are of opinion that it has been from all eternity, is mortal, and renewed again by several vicissitudes; calling Solomon and Isaiah to witness; to evade those oppositions, that God has once been a creator without a creature; that he has had nothing to do, that he got rid of that idleness by putting his hand to this work; and that consequently he is subject to change. In the most famous of the Greek schools the world is taken for a god, made by another god greater than he, and composed of a body, and a soul fixed in his centre, and dilating himself by musical numbers to his circumference; divine, infinitely happy, and infinitely great, infinitely wise and eternal; in him are other gods, the sea, the earth, the stars, who entertain one another with an harmonious and perpetual agitation and divine dance, sometimes meeting, sometimes retiring from one another; concealing and discovering themselves; changing their order, one while before, and another behind. Heraclitus was positive that the world was composed of fire; and, by the order of destiny, was one day to be enflamed and consumed in fire, and then to be again renewed. And Apuleius says of men: Sigillatim mortales, cunctim perpetui. "That they are mortal in particular, and immortal in general." Alexander writ to his mother the narration of an Egyptian priest, drawn from their monuments, testifying the antiquity of that nation to be infinite, and comprising the birth and progress of other countries. Cicero and Diodorus say that in their time the Chaldees kept a register of four hundred thousand and odd years, Aristotle, Pliny, and others, that Zoroaster flourished six thousand years before Plato's time. Plato says that they of the city of Sais have records in writing of eight thousand years; and that the city of Athens was built a thousand years before the said city of Sais; Epicurus, that at the same time things are here in the posture we see, they are alike and in the same manner in several other worlds; which he would have delivered with greater assurance, had he seen the similitude and concordance of the new discovered world of the West Indies with ours, present and past, in so many strange examples.

In earnest, considering what is come to our knowledge from the course of this terrestrial polity, I have often wondered to see in so vast a distance of places and times such a concurrence of so great a number of popular and wild opinions, and of savage manners and beliefs, which by no means seem to proceed from our natural meditation. The human mind is a great worker of miracles! But this relation has, moreover, I know not what of extraordinary in it; 'tis found to be in names, also, and a thousand other things; for they found nations there (that, for aught we know, never heard of us) where circumcision was in use; where there were states and great civil governments maintained by women only, without men; where our fasts and Lent were represented, to which was added abstinence from women; where our crosses were several ways in repute; here they were made use of to honour and adorn their sepultures, there they were erected, and particularly that of St Andrew, to protect themselves from nocturnal visions, and to lay upon the cradles of infants against enchantments; elsewhere there was found one of wood, of very great height, which was adored for the god of rain, and this a great way in the interior; there was seen an express image of our penance priests, the use of mitres, the celibacy of priests, the art of divination by the entrails of sacrificed beasts, abstinence from all sorts of flesh and fish in their diet, the manner of priests officiating in a particular and not a vulgar language; and this fancy, that the first god was driven away by a second, his younger brother; that they were created with all sorts of necessaries and conveniences, which have since been in a degree taken from them for their sins, their territory changed, and their natural condition made worse; that they were of old overwhelmed by the inundation of water from heaven; that but few families escaped, who retired into caves on high mountains, the mouths of which they stopped so that the waters could not get in, having shut up, together with themselves, several sorts of animals; that when they perceived the rain to cease they sent out dogs, which returning clean and wet, they judged that the water was not much abated; afterwards sending out others, and seeing them return dirty, they issued out to repeople the world, which they found only full of serpents. In one place we met with the belief of a day of judgment; insomuch that they were marvellously displeased at the Spaniards for discomposing the bones of the dead, in rifling the sepultures for riches, saying that those bones so disordered could not easily rejoin; the traffic by exchange, and no other way; fairs and markets for that end; dwarfs and deformed people for the ornament of the tables of princes; the use of falconry, according to the nature of their hawks; tyrannical subsidies; nicety in gardens; dancing, tumbling tricks, music of instruments, coats of arms, tennis-courts, dice and lotteries, wherein they are sometimes so eager and hot as to stake themselves and their liberty; physic, no otherwise than by charms; the way of writing in cypher; the belief of only one first man, the father of all nations; the adoration of one God, who formerly lived a man in perfect virginity, fasting, and penitence, preaching the laws of nature, and the ceremonies of religion, and that vanished from the world without a natural death; the theory of giants; the custom of making themselves drunk with their beverages, and drinking to the utmost; religious ornaments painted with bones and dead men's skulls; surplices, holy water sprinkled; wives and servants, who present themselves with emulation, burnt and interred with the dead husband or master; a law by which the eldest succeeds to all the estate, no part being left for the younger but obedience; the custom that, upon promotion to a certain office of great authority, the promoted is to take upon him a new name, and to leave that which he had before; another to strew lime upon the knee of the new-born child, with these words:

"From dust thou earnest, and to dust thou must return;" as also the art of augury. The vain shadows of our religion, which are observable in some of these examples, are testimonies of its dignity and divinity. It is not only in some sort insinuated into all the infidel nations on this side of the world, by a certain imitation, but in these barbarians also, as by a common and supernatural inspiration; for we find there the belief of purgatory, but of a new form; that which we give to the fire they give to the cold, and imagine that souls are purged and punished by the rigour of an excessive coldness. And this example puts me in mind of another pleasant diversity; for as there were there some people who delighted to unmuffle the ends of their instruments, and clipped off the prepuce after the Mahometan and Jewish manner; there were others who made so great conscience of laying it bare, that they carefully pursed it up with little strings to keep that end from peeping into the air; and of this other diversity, that whereas we, to honour kings and festivals, put on the best clothes we have; in some regions, to express their disparity and submission to their king, his subjects present themselves before him in their vilest habits, and entering his palace, throw some old tattered garment over their better apparel, to the end that all the lustre and ornament may solely be in him. But to proceed:—

If nature enclose within the bounds of her ordinary progress the beliefs, judgments, and opinions of men, as well as all other things; if they have their revolution, their season, their birth and death, like cabbage plants; if the heavens agitate and rule them at their pleasure, what magisterial and permanent authority do we attribute to them? If we experimentally see that the form of our beings depends upon the air, upon the climate, and upon the soil, where we are born, and not only the colour, the stature, the complexion, and the countenances, but moreover the very faculties of the soul itself: Et plaga codi non solum ad robor corporum, sed etiam anirum facit: "The climate is of great efficacy, not only to the strength of bodies, but to that of souls also," says Vegetius; and that the goddess who founded the city of Athens chose to situate it in a temperature of air fit to make men prudent, as the Egyptian priests told Solon: Athenis tenue colum; ex quo etiam acutiores putantur Attici; crassum Thebis; itaque pingues Thebani, et valentes: "The air of Athens is subtle and thin; whence also the Athenians are reputed to be more acute; and at Thebes more gross and thick; wherefore the Thebans are looked upon as more heavy-witted and more strong." In such sort that, as fruits and animals grow different, men are also more or less warlike, just, temperate, and docile; here given to wine, elsewhere to theft or uncleanness; here inclined to superstition, elsewhere to unbelief; in one place to liberty, in another to servitude; capable of one science or of one art, dull or ingenious, obedient or mutinous, good or bad, according as the place where they are seated inclines them; and assume a new complexion, if removed, like trees, which was the reason why Cyrus would not grant the Persians leave to quit their rough and craggy country to remove to another more pleasant and even, saying, that fertile and tender soils made men effeminate and soft. If we see one while one art and one belief flourish, and another while another, through some celestial influence; such an age to produce such natures, and to incline mankind to such and such a propension, the spirits of men one while gay and another gray, like our fields, what becomes of all those fine prerogatives we so soothe ourselves withal? Seeing that a wise man may be mistaken, and a hundred men and a hundred nations, nay, that even human nature itself, as we believe, is many ages wide in one thing or another, what assurances have we that she should cease to be mistaken, or that in this very age of ours she is not so?

Methinks that amongst other testimonies of our imbecility, this ought not to be forgotten, that man cannot, by his own wish and desire, find out what he wants; that not in fruition only, but in imagination and wish, we cannot agree about what we would have to satisfy and content us. Let us leave it to our own thought to cut out and make up at pleasure; it cannot so much as covet what is proper for it, and satisfy itself:—

> Quid enim ratione timemus,
>
> Aut cupimus? Quid tain dextro pede concipis, ut te
>
> Conatus non poniteat, votique peracti?

> "For what, with reason, do we speak or shun,
>
> What plan, how happily soe'r begun,
>
> That, when achieved, we do not wish undone?"

And therefore it was that Socrates only begged of the gods that they would give him what they knew to be best for him; and the private and public prayer of the Lacedemonians was simply for good and useful things, referring the choice and election of them to the discretion of the Supreme Power:—

> Conjugium petimus, partumqu uxoris; at illis
>
> Notum, qui pueri, qualisque futura sit uxor:

"We ask for Wives and children; they above

Know only, when we have them, what they'll prove;"

and Christians pray to God, "Thy will be done," that they may not fall into the inconvenience the poet feigns of King Midas. He prayed to the gods that all he touched might be turned into gold; his prayer was heard; his wine was gold, his bread was gold, the feathers of his bed, his shirt, his clothes, were all gold, so that he found himself overwhelmed with the fruition of his desire, and endowed with an intolerable benefit, and was fain to unpray his prayers.

Attonitus novitate mali, divesque, miserque,

Effugere optt opes, et, qu modo voverat, odit.

"Astonished at the strangeness of the ill,

To be so rich, yet miserable still;

He wishes now he could his wealth evade,

And hates the thing for which before he prayed."

To instance in myself: being young, I desired of fortune, above all things, the order of St. Michael, which was then the utmost distinction of honour amongst the French nobles, and very rare. She pleasantly gratified my longing; instead of raising me, and lifting me up from my own place to attain to it, she was much kinder to me; for she brought it so low, and made it so cheap, that it stooped down to my shoulders, and lower. Cleobis and Bito, Trophonius and Agamedes, having requested, the first of their goddess, the last of their god, a recompense worthy of their piety, had death for a reward; so differing from ours are heavenly opinions concerning what is fit for us. God might grant us riches, honours, life, and even health, to our own hurt; for every thing that is pleasing to us is not always good for us. If he sends us death, or an increase of sickness, instead of a cure, Vvrga tua et baculus, tuus ipsa me consolata sunt. "Thy rod and thy staff have comforted me," he does it by the rule of his providence, which better and more certainly discerns what is proper for us than we can do; and we ought to take it in good part, as coming from a wise and most friendly hand

Si consilium vis:

Permittee ipsis expendere numinibus, quid

Conveniat nobis, rebusque sit utile nostris...

Carior est illis homo quam sibi;

"If thou'lt be rul'd, to th' gods thy fortunes trust,

Their thoughts are wise, their dispensations just.

What best may profit or delight they know,

And real good, for fancied bliss, bestow;

With eyes of pity, they our frailties scan,

More dear to them, than to himself, is man;"

for to require of him honours and commands, is to require 'that he may throw you into a battle, set you upon a cast at dice, or something of the like nature, whereof the issue is to you unknown, and the fruit doubtful.

There is no dispute so sharp and violent amongst the philosophers, as about the question of the sovereign good of man; whence, by the calculation of Varro, rose two hundred and eighty-eight sects. Qui autem de summo bono dissentit, de tot philosophies ratione disputt. "For whoever enters into controversy concerning the supreme good, disputes upon the whole matter of philosophy."

Trs mihi conviv prope dissentire videntur,

Poscentes vario mul turn divers a palato;

Quid dem? Quid non dem? Renuis tu quod jubet alter;

Quod petis, id sane est invisum acidumque duobus;

"I have three guests invited to a feast,

And all appear to have a different taste;

What shall I give them? What shall I refuse?

What one dislikes the other two shall choose;

And e'en the very dish you like the best

Is acid or insipid to the rest:"

nature should say the same to their contests and debates. Some say that our well-being lies in virtue, others in pleasure, others in submitting to nature; one in knowledge, another in being exempt from pain, another in not suffering ourselves to be carried away by appearances; and this fancy seems to have some relation to that of the ancient Pythagoras,

>   Nil admirari, prope res est una, Numici,

>   Solaque, qu possit facere et servare beatum:

> "Not to admire's the only art I know
>
> Can make us happy, and can keep us so;"

which is the drift of the Pyrrhonian sect; Aristotle attributes the admiring nothing to magnanimity; and Arcesilaus said, that constancy and a right inflexible state of judgment were the true good, and consent and application the sin and evil; and there, it is true, in being thus positive, and establishing a certain axiom, he quitted Pyrrhonism; for the' Pyrrhonians, when they say that ataraxy, which is the immobility of judgment, is the sovereign good, do not design to speak it affirmatively; but that the same motion of soul which makes them avoid precipices, and take shelter from the cold, presents them such a fancy, and makes them refuse another.

How much do I wish that, whilst I live, either some other or Justus Lipsius, the most learned man now living, of a most polite and judicious understanding, truly resembling my Turnebus, had both the will and health, and leisure sufficient, carefully and conscientiously to collect into a register, according to their divisions and classes, as many as are to be found, of the opinions of the ancient philosophers, about the subject of our being and manners, their controversies, the succession and reputation of sects; with the application of the lives of the authors and their disciples to their own precepts, in memorable accidents, and upon exemplary occasions. What a beautiful and useful work that would be!

As to what remains, if it be from ourselves that we are to extract the rules of our manners, upon what a confusion do we throw ourselves! For that which our reason advises us to, as the most likely, is generally for every one to obey the laws of his country, as was the advice of Socrates, inspired, as he says, by a divine counsel; and by that, what would it say, but that our duty has no other rule but what is accidental? Truth ought to have a like and universal visage; if man could know equity and justice that had a body and a true being, he would not fetter it to the conditions of this country or that; it would not be from the whimsies of the Persians or Indians that virtue would receive its form. There is nothing more subject to perpetual agitation than the laws; since I was born, I have known those of the English, our neighbours, three or four times changed, not only in matters of civil regimen, which is the only thing wherein constancy may be dispensed with, but in the most important subject that can be, namely, religion, at which I am the more troubled and ashamed, because it is a nation with whom those of my province have formerly had so great familiarity and acquaintance, that there yet remains in my house some footsteps of our ancient kindred; and here with us at home, I have known a thing that was capital to become lawful; and we that hold of others are likewise, according to the chance of war, in a possibility of being one day found guilty of high-treason, both divine and human, should the justice of our arms fall into the power of injustice, and, after a few years' possession, take a quite contrary being. How could that ancient god more clearly accuse the ignorance of human knowledge concerning the divine Being, and give men to understand that their religion was but a thing of their own contrivance, useful as a bond to their society, than declaring as he did to those who came to his tripod for instruction, that every one's true worship was that which he found in use in the place where he chanced to be? O God, what infinite obligation have we to the bounty of our sovereign Creator, for having disabused our belief from these wandering and arbitrary devotions, and for having seated it upon the eternal foundation of his holy word? But what then will philosophers say to us in this necessity? "That we follow the laws of our country;" that is to say, this floating sea of the opinions of a republic, or a prince, that will paint out justice for me in as many colours, and form it as many ways as there are changes of passions in themselves; I cannot suffer my judgment to be so flexible. What kind of virtue is that which I see one day in repute, and that to-morrow shall be in none, and which the crossing of a river makes a crime? What sort of truth can that be, which these mountains limit to us, and make a lie to all the world beyond them?

But they are pleasant, when, to give some certainty to the laws, they say, that there are some firm, perpetual, and immovable, which they call natural, that are imprinted in human kind by the condition of their own proper being; and of these some reckon three, some four, some more, some less; a sign that it is a mark as doubtful as the rest Now they are so unfortunate, (for what can I call it else but misfortune that, of so infinite a number of laws, there should not be found one at least that fortune and the temerity of chance has suffered to be universally received by the consent of all nations?) they are, I say, so miserable, that of these three or four select laws, there is not so much as one that is not contradicted and disowned, not only by one nation, but by many. Now, the only likely sign, by which they can argue or infer some natural laws, is the universality of approbation; for we should, without doubt, follow with a common consent that which nature had truly ordained us; and not only every nation, but every private man, would resent the force and violence that any one should do him who would tempt him to any thing contrary to this law. But let them produce me one of this condition. Proctagoras and Aristo gave no other essence to the justice of laws than the authority and opinion of the legislator; and that, these laid aside, the honest and the good lost their qualities, and remained empty names of indifferent things; Thrasymachus, in Plato, is of opinion that there is no other right but the convenience of the superior. There is not any thing wherein the world is so various as in laws and customs; such a thing is abominable here which is elsewhere in esteem, as in Lacedemon dexterity in stealing; marriages between near relations, are capitally interdicted amongst us; they are elsewhere in honour:—

Gentes esse ferantur,

In quibus et nato genitrix, et nata parenti

Jungitur, et pietas geminato crescit amore;

"There are some nations in the world, 'tis said,

Where fathers daughters, sons their mothers wed;

And their affections thereby higher rise,

More firm and constant by these double ties;"

the murder of infants, the murder of fathers, the community of wives, traffic of robberies, license in all sorts of voluptuousness; in short, there is nothing so extreme that is not allowed by the custom of some nation or other.

It is credible that there are natural laws for us, as we see them in other creatures; but they are lost in us, this fine human reason everywhere so insinuating itself to govern and command, as to shuffle and confound the face of things, according to its own vanity and inconstancy: Nihil itaque amplius nostrum est; quod nostrum dico, artis est: "Therefore nothing is any more truly ours; what we call ours belongs to art." Subjects have divers lustres and divers considerations, and thence the diversity of opinions principally proceeds; one nation considers a subject in one aspect, and stops there: another takes it in a different point of view.

There is nothing of greater horror to be imagined than for a man to eat his father; and yet the people, whose ancient custom it was so to do, looked upon it as a testimony of piety and affection, seeking thereby to give their progenitors the most worthy and honourable sepulture; storing up in themselves, and as it were in their own marrow, the bodies and relics of their fathers; and in some sort regenerating them by transmutation into their living flesh, by means of nourishment and digestion. It is easy to consider what a cruelty and abomination it must have appeared to men possessed and imbued with this snperstition to throw their fathers' remains to the corruption of the earth, and the nourishment of beasts and worms.

Lycurgus considered in theft the vivacity, diligence, boldness, and dexterity of purloining any thing from our neighbours, and the benefit that redounded to the public that every one should look more narrowly to the conservation of what was his own; and believed that, from this double institution of assaulting and defending, advantage was to be made for military discipline (which was the principal science and virtue to which he would inure that nation), of greater consideration than the disorder and injustice of taking another man's goods.

Dionysius, the tyrant, offered Plato a robe of the Persian fashion, long, damasked, and perfumed; Plato refused it, saying, "That being born a man, he would not willingly dress himself in women's clothes;" but Aristippus accepted it with this answer, "That no accoutrement could corrupt a chaste courage." His friends reproaching him with meanness of spirit, for laying it no more to heart that Dionysius had spit in his face, "Fishermen," said he, "suffer themselves to be drenched with the waves of the sea from head to foot to catch a gudgeon." Diogenes was washing cabbages, and seeing him pass by, "If thou couldst live on cabbage," said he, "thou wouldst not fawn upon a tyrant;" to whom Aristippus replied, "And if thou knewest how to live amongst men, thou wouldst not be washing cabbages." Thus reason finds appearances for divers effects; 'tis a pot with two ears that a man may take by the right or left:—

   Bellum, o terra hospita, portas:

Bello armantur eqni; bellum hc armenta minantur.

Sed tamen idem olim curru succedere sueti

Quadrupedes, et frena jugo concordia ferre;

Spes est pacis.

   "War, war is threatened from this foreign ground

(My father cried), where warlike steeds are found.

Yet, since reclaimed, to chariots they submit,

And bend to stubborn yokes, and champ the bit,

Peace may succeed to war."

Solon, being lectured by his friends not to shed powerless and unprofitable tears for the death of his son, "It is for that reason that I the more justly shed them," said he, "because they are powerless and unprofitable." Socrates's wife exasperated her grief by this circumstance: "Oh, how unjustly do these wicked judges put him to death!" "Why," replied he, "hadst thou rather they should execute me justly?" We have our ears bored; the Greeks looked upon that as a mark of slavery. We retire in private to enjoy our wives; the Indians do it in public. The Scythians immolated strangers in their temples; elsewhere temples were a refuge:—

Inde furor vulgi, quod numina vicinorum

Odit quisque locus, cum solos credat habendos

Esse deos, quos ipse colit.

"Thus 'tis the popular fury that creates

That all their neighbours' gods each nation hates;

Each thinks its own the genuine; in a word,

The only deities to be adored."

I have heard of a judge who, coming upon a sharp conflict betwixt Bartolus and Aldus, and some point controverted with many contrarieties, writ in the margin of his book, "a question for a friend;" that is to say, that truth was there so controverted and disputed that in a like cause he might favour which of the parties he thought fit 'Twas only for want of wit that he did not write "a question for a friend" throughout. The advocates and judges of our times find bias enough in all causes to accommodate them to what they themselves think fit. In so infinite a science, depending upon the authority of so many opinions, and so arbitrary a subject, it cannot be but that of necessity an extreme confusion of judgments must arise; there is hardly any suit so clear wherein opinions do not very much differ; what one court has determined one way another determines quite contrary, and itself contrary to that at another time. Of which we see very frequent examples, owing to that practice admitted amongst us, and which is a marvellous blemish to the ceremonious authority and lustre of our justice, of not abiding by one sentence, but running from judge to judge, and court to court, to decide one and the same cause.

As to the liberty of philosophical opinions concerning vice and virtue, 'tis not necessary to be insisted upon; therein are found many opinions that are better concealed than published to weak minds. Arcesilaus said, "That in venery it was no matter where, or with whom, it was committed:" Et obsccenas voluptates, si natura requirit, non genere, aut loco, aut ordine, sed forma, otate, jigur, metiendas Epicurus putat.... ne amores quidem sanctos a sapiente alienos esse arbitrantur.... Queeramus, ad quam usque otatem juvenes amandi sint. "And obscene pleasures, if nature requires them," Epicurus thinks, "are not to be measured either by race, kind, place, or rank, but by age, shape, and beauty.... Neither are sacred loves thought to be foreign to wise men;... we are to inquire till what age young men are to be loved." These last two stoical quotations, and the reproach that Dicarchus threw into the teeth of Plato himself, upon this account, show how much the soundest philosophy indulges licenses and excesses very remote from common custom.

Laws derive their authority from possession and custom. 'Tis dangerous to trace them back to their beginning; they grow great, and ennoble themselves, like our rivers, by running on; but follow them upward to their source, 'tis but a little spring, scarce discernable,

that swells thus, and thus fortifies itself by growing old. Do but consult the ancient considerations that gave the first motion to this famous torrent, so full of dignity, awe, and reverence, you will find them so light and weak that it is no wonder if these people, who weigh and reduce every thing to reason, and who admit nothing by authority, or upon trust, have their judgments often very remote, and differing from those of the public. It is no wonder if people, who take their pattern from the first image of nature, should in most of their opinions swerve from the common path; as, for example, few amongst them would have approved of the strict conditions of our marriages, and most of them have been for having wives in common, and without obligation; they would refuse our ceremonies. Chrysippus said, "That a philosopher would make a dozen somersaults, aye, and without his breeches, for a dozen of olives." That philosopher would hardly have advised Clisthenes to have refused Hippoclides the fair Agarista his daughter, for having seen him stand on his head upon a table. Metrocles somewhat indiscreetly broke wind backwards while in disputation, in the presence of a great auditory in his school, and kept himself hid in his own house for shame, till Crates coming to visit him, and adding to his consolations and reasons the example of his own liberty, by falling to try with him who should sound most, cured him of that scruple, and withal drew him to his own stoical sect, more free than that more reserved one of the Peripatetics, of which he had been till then. That which we call decency, not to dare to do that in public which is decent enough to do in private, the Stoics call foppery; and to mince it, and to be so modest as to conceal and disown what nature, custom, and our desires publish and proclaim of our actions, they reputed a vice. The other thought it was to undervalue the mysteries of Venus to draw them out of the private oratory, to expose them to the view of the people; and that to bring them out from behind the curtain was to debase them. Modesty is a thing of weight; secrecy, reservation, and circumspection, are parts of esteem. Pleasure did very ingeniously when, under the mask of virtue, she sued not to be prostituted in the open streets, trodden under foot, and exposed to the public view, wanting the dignity and convenience of her private cabinets. Hence some say that to put down public stews is not only to disperse fornication into all places, that was confined to one, but moreover, by the difficulty, to incite wild and idle people to this vice:—

   Mochus es Aufidi, qui vir,

   Scvine, fuisti:

   Rivalis fuerat qui tuus, ille vir est.

   Cur alina placet tibi, qu tua non placet uxor?

   Numquid securus non potes arrigere?

This experience diversifies itself in a thousand examples:—

> Nullus in urbe fuit tot, qui tangere vellet
>
> Uxorem gratis, Cciliane, tuam,
>
> Dum licuit: sed nunc, positis custodibus, ingens
>
> Turba fututorum est. Ingeniosus homo es.

A philosopher being taken in the very act, and asked what he was doing, coldly replied, "I am planting man;" no more blushing to be so caught than if they had found him planting garlic.

It is, I suppose, out of tenderness and respect to the natural modesty of mankind that a great and religious author is of opinion that this act is so necessarily obliged to privacy and shame that he cannot persuade himself there could be any absolute performance in those impudent embraces of the Cynics, but that they contented themselves to represent lascivious gestures only, to maintain the impudence of their school's profession; and that, to eject what shame had withheld and restrained, it was afterward necessary for them to withdraw into the shade. But he had not thoroughly examined their debauches; for Diogenes, playing the beast with himself in public, wished, in the presence of all that saw him, that he could fill his belly by that exercise. To those who asked him why he did not find out a more commodious place to eat in than in the open street, he made answer, "Because I am hungry in the open street." The women philosophers who mixed with their sect, mixed also with their persons, in all places, without reservation; and Hipparchia was not received into Crates's society, but upon condition that she should, in all things, follow the practice and customs of his rule. These philosophers set a great price upon virtue, and renounce all other discipline but the moral; and yet, in all their actions, they attributed the sovereign authority to the election of their sage, and above the laws; and gave no other curb to voluptuousness but moderation only, and the conservation of the liberty of others.

Heraclitus and Protagoras, forasmuch as wine seemed bitter to the sick, and pleasant to the sound, the rudder crooked in the water, and straight when out, and such like contrary appearances as are found in subjects, argued thence that all subjects had, in themselves, the causes of these appearances; and there was some bitterness in the wine which had some sympathy with the sick man's taste, and the rudder some bending quality sympathizing with him that looks upon it in the water; and so of all the rest; which is to say, that all is in all things, and, consequently, nothing in any one; for, where all is, there is nothing.

This opinion put me in mind of the experience we have that there is no sense or aspect of any thing, whether bitter or sweet, straight or crooked, that the human mind does not find out in the writings it undertakes to tumble over. Into the cleanest, purest, and most perfect words that can possibly be, how many lies and falsities have we suggested! What heresy has not there found ground and testimony sufficient to make itself embraced and defended! 'Tis for this that the authors of such errors will never depart from proof of the testimony of the interpretation of words. A person of dignity, who would approve to me, by authority, the search of the philosopher's stone, wherein he was head over ears engaged, lately alleged to me at least five or six passages of the Bible upon which, he said, he first founded his attempt, for the discharge of his conscience (for he is a divine); and, in truth, the idea was not only pleasant, but, moreover, very well accommodated to the defence of this fine science.

By this way the reputation of divining fables is acquired. There is no fortune-teller, if we have this authority, but, if a man will take the pains to tumble and toss, and narrowly to peep into all the folds and glosses of his words, he may make him, like the Sibyls, say what he will. There are so many ways of interpretation that it will be hard but that, either obliquely or in a direct line, an ingenious wit will find out, in every subject, some air that will serve for his purpose; therefore we find a cloudy and ambiguous style in so frequent and ancient use. Let the author but make himself master of that, to busy posterity about his predictions, which not only his own parts, but the accidental favour of the matter itself, may do for him; and, as to the rest, express himself, whether after a foolish or a subtle manner, somewhat obscurely or contradictorily, 'tis no matter;—a number of wits, shaking and sifting him, will bring out a great many several forms, either according to his meaning, or collateral, or contrary, to it, which will all redound to his honour; he will see himself enriched by the means of his disciples, like the regents of colleges by their pupils yearly presents. This it is which has given reputation to many things of no worth at all; that has brought several writings in vogue, and given them the fame of containing all sorts of matter can be desired; one and the same thing receiving a thousand and a thousand images and various considerations; nay, as many as we please.

Is it possible that Homer could design to say all that we make him say, and that he designed so many and so various figures, as that the divines, law-givers, captains, philosophers, and all sorts of men who treat of sciences, how variously and opposite soever, should indifferently quote him, and support their arguments by his authority, as the sovereign lord and master of all offices, works, and artisans, and counsellor-general of all enterprises? Whoever has had occasion for oracles and predictions has there found sufficient to serve his turn. 'Tis a wonder how many and how admirable concurrences an intelligent person, and a particular friend of mine, has there found out in favour of our religion; and cannot easily be put out of the conceit that it was Homer's design; and yet he is as well acquainted with this author as any man whatever of his time. And what he has found in favour of our religion there, very many anciently have found in favour of theirs. Do but observe how Plato is tumbled and tossed about; every one ennobling his own opinions by applying him to himself, and making him take what side they please. They draw him in, and engage him in all the new opinions the world receives; and make him, according to the different course of things, differ from himself; every one makes him disavow, according to his own sense, the manners and customs lawful in his age, because they are unlawful in ours; and all this with vivacity and power, according to the force and sprightliness of the wit of the interpreter. From the same foundation that Heraclitus and this sentence of his had, "that all things had in them those forms that we discern," Democritus drew quite a contrary conclusion,—"that objects have in them nothing that we discern in them;" and because honey is sweet to one and bitter to another, he thence argued that it was neither sweet nor bitter. The Pyrrhonians would say that they knew not whether it is sweet or bitter, or whether the one or the other, or both; for these always gained the highest point of dubitation. The Cyrenaics held that nothing was perceptible from without, and that that only was perceptible that inwardly touched us, as pain and pleasure; acknowledging neither sound nor colour, but certain affections only that we receive from them; and that man's judgment had no other seat Protagoras believed that "what seems true to every one, is true to every one." The Epicureans lodged all judgment in the senses, and in the knowledge of things, and in pleasure. Plato would have the judgment of truth, and truth itself, derived from opinions and the senses, to belong to the wit and cogitation.

This discourse has put me upon the consideration of the senses, in which lies the greatest foundation and Prof of our ignorance. Whatsoever is known, is doubtless known by the faculty of the knower; for, seeing the judgment proceeds from the operation of him that judges, 'tis reason that this operation be performed by his means and will, not by the constraint of another; as it would happen if we knew things by the power, and according to the law of their essence. Now all knowledge is conveyed to us by the senses; they are our masters:—

> Via qua munita fidei
>
> Proxima fert humanum in pectus, templaque mentis;

> "It is the surest path that faith can find
>
> By which to enter human heart and mind."

Science begins by them, and is resolved into them. After all, we should know no more than a stone if we did not know there is sound, odour, light, taste, measure, weight, softness, hardness, sharpness, colour, smoothness, breadth, and depth; these are the platforms and principles of the structure of all our knowledge; and, according to some, science is nothing else but sense. He that could make me contradict the senses, would have me by the throat; he could not make me go further back. The senses are the beginning and the end of human knowledge:—

> Invenies primis ab sensibns esse creatam
>
> Notitiam veil; neque sensus posse refelli....
>
> Quid majore fide porro, quam sensus, haberi Debet?

> "Of truth, whate'er discoveries are made,

Are by the senses to us first conveyed;

Nor will one sense be baffled; for on what

Can we rely more safely than on that?"

Let us attribute to them the least we can, we must, however, of necessity grant them this, that it is by their means and mediation that all our instruction is directed. Cicero says, that Chrysippus having attempted to extenuate the force and virtue of the senses, presented to himself arguments and so vehement oppositions to the contrary that he could not satisfy himself therein; whereupon Cameades, who maintained the contrary side, boasted that he would make use of the very words and arguments of Chrysippus to controvert and confute him, and therefore thus cried out against him: "O miserable! thy force has destroyed thee." There can be nothing absurd to a greater degree than to maintain that fire does not warm, that light does not shine, and that there is no weight nor solidity in iron, which are things conveyed to us by the senses; neither is there belief nor knowledge in man that can be compared to that for certainty.

The first consideration I have upon the subject of the senses is that I make a doubt whether or no man be furnished with all natural senses. I see several animals who live an entire and perfect life, some without sight, others without hearing; who knows whether to us also one, two, three, or many other senses may not be wanting? For if any one be wanting, our examination cannot discover the defect. 'Tis the privilege of the senses to be the utmost limit of our discovery; there is nothing beyond them that can assist us in exploration, not so much as one sense in the discovery of another:—

An poterunt oculos aures reprehendere? an aures

Tactus an hunc porro tactum sapor argnet oris?

An confutabunt nares, oculive revincent?

"Can ears the eyes, the touch the ears, correct?

Or is that touch by tasting to be check'd?

Or th' other senses, shall the nose or eyes

Confute in their peculiar faculties?"

They all make the extremest limits of our ability:—

Seorsum cuique potestas Divisa est, sua vis cuique est,

> "Each has its power distinctly and alone,
>
> And every sense's power is its own."

It is impossible to make a man naturally blind conceive that he does not see; impossible to make him desire sight, or to regret his defect; for which reason we ought not to derive any assurance from the soul's being contented and satisfied with those we have; considering that it cannot be sensible herein of its infirmity and imperfection, if there be any such thing. It is impossible to say any thing to this blind man, either by reasoning, argument, or similitude, that can possess his imagination with any apprehension of light, colour, or sight; there's nothing remains behind that can push on the senses to evidence. Those that are born blind, whom we hear wish they could see, it is not that they understand what they desire; they have learned from us that they want something; that there is something to be desired that we have, which they can name indeed and speak of its effect and consequences; but yet they know not what it is, nor apprehend it at all.

I have seen a gentleman of a good family who was born blind, or at least blind from such an age that he knows not what sight is; who is so little sensible of his defect that he makes use as we do of words proper for seeing, and applies them after a manner wholly particular and his own. They brought him a child to which he was god-father, which, having taken into his arms, "Good God," said he, "what a fine child! How beautiful to look upon! what a pretty face it has!" He will say, like one of us, "This room has a very fine prospect;—it is clear weather;—the sun shines bright." And moreover, being that hunting, tennis, and butts are our exercises, and he has heard so, he has taken a liking to them, will ride a-hunting, and believes he has as good share of the sport as we have; and will express himself as angry or pleased as the best of us all, and yet knows nothing of it but by the ear. One cries out to him, "Here's a hare!" when he is upon some even plain where he may safely ride; and afterwards, when they tell him, "The hare is killed," he will be as overjoyed and proud of it as he hears others say they are. He will take a tennis-ball in his left hand and strike it away with the racket; he will shoot with a harquebuss at random, and is contented with what his people tell him, that he is over, or wide.

Who knows whether all human kind commit not the like absurdity, for want of some sense, and that through this default the greatest part of the face of things is concealed from us? What do we know but that the difficulties which we find in several works of nature proceed hence; and that several effects of animals, which exceed our capacity, are not produced by faculty of some sense that we are defective in? and whether some of them have not by this means a life more full and entire than ours? We seize an apple with all our senses; we there find redness, smoothness, odour, and sweetness; but it may have other virtues besides these, as to heat or binding, which no sense of ours can have any reference unto. Is it not likely that there are sensitive faculties in nature that are fit to judge of and to discern those which we call the occult properties in several things, as for the loadstone to attract iron; and that the want of such faculties is the cause that we are ignorant of the true essence of such things? 'Tis perhaps some particular sense that gives cocks to understand what hour it is at midnight, and when it grows to be towards day, and that makes them crow accordingly; that teaches chickens, before they have any experience of the matter, to fear a sparrow-hawk, and not a goose or a peacock, though birds of a much larger size; that cautions them against the hostile quality the cat has against them, and makes them not to fear a dog; to arm themselves against the mewing, a kind of flattering voice, of the one, and not against the barking, a shrill and threatening voice, of the other; that teaches wasps, ants, and rats, to fall upon the best pear and the best cheese before they have tasted them, and inspires the stag, elephant, and serpent, with the knowledge of a certain herb proper for their cure. There is no sense that has not a mighty dominion, and that does not by its power introduce an infinite number of knowledges. If we were defective in the intelligence of sounds, of harmony, and of the voice, it would cause an unimaginable confusion in all the rest of our science; for, besides what belongs to the proper effect of every sense, how many arguments, consequences, and conclusions do we draw to other things, by comparing one sense with another? Let an understanding man imagine human nature originally produced without the sense of seeing, and consider what ignorance and trouble such a defect would bring upon him, what a darkness and blindness in the soul; he will then see by that of how great importance to the knowledge of truth the privation of such another sense, or of two or three, should we be so deprived, would be. We have formed a truth by the consultation and concurrence of our five senses; but perhaps we should have the consent and contribution of eight or ten to make a certain discovery of it in its essence.

The sects that controvert the knowledge of man do it principally by the uncertainty and weakness of our senses; for since all knowledge is by their means and mediation conveyed unto us, if they fail in their report, if they corrupt or alter what they bring us from without, if the light which by them creeps into the soul be obscured in the passage, we have nothing else to hold by. From this extreme difficulty all these fancies proceed: "That every subject has in itself all we there find. That it has nothing in it of what we think we there find;" and that of the Epicureans, "That the sun is no bigger than 'tis judged by our sight to be:—"

    Quidquid id est, nihilo fertur majore figura,

    Quam nostris oculis quam cemimus, esse videtur:

    "But be it what it will in our esteems,

    It is no bigger than to us it seems:"

that the appearances which represent a body great to him that is near, and less to him that is more remote, are both true:—

Nee tamen hic oculos falli concedimus hilum....

Proinde animi vitium hoc oculis adfingere noli:

"Yet that the eye's deluded we deny;

Charge not the mind's faults, therefore, on the eye:"

"and, resolutely, that there is no deceit in the senses; that we are to lie at their mercy, and seek elsewhere reasons to excuse the difference and contradictions we there find, even to the inventing of lies and other flams, if it come to that, rather than accuse the senses." Timagoras vowed that, by pressing or turning his eye, he could never perceive the light of the candle to double, and that the seeming so proceeded from the vice of opinion, and not from the instrument. The most absurd of all absurdities, with the Epicureans, is to deny the force and effect of the senses:—

Proinde, quod in quoquo est his visum tempore, verum est

Et, si non potuit ratio dissolvere causam,

Cur ea, qu fuerint juxtim quadrata, procul sint

Visa rotunda; tamen prstat rationis egentem

Beddere mendose causas utriusque figur,

Quam manibus manifesta suis emittere ququam,

Et violare fidem primam, et convellere tota

Fundamenta, quibus nixatur vita salusque:

Non modo enim ratio ruat omnis, vita quoque ipsa

Concidat extemplo, nisi credere sensibus ausis,

Procipitesque locos vitare, et ctera, qu sint

In genere hoc fugienda.

"That what we see exists I will maintain,

And if our feeble reason can't explain

Why things seem square when they are very near,

And at a greater distance round appear;

'Tis better yet, for him that's at a pause,

'T' assign to either figure a false cause,

Than shock his faith, and the foundations rend

On which our safety and our life depend:

For reason not alone, but life and all,

Together will with sudden ruin fall;

Unless we trust our senses, nor despise

To shun the various dangers that arise."

This so desperate and unphilosophical advice expresses only this,—that human knowledge cannot support itself but by reason unreasonable, foolish, and mad; but that it is yet better that man, to set a greater value upon himself, make use of any other remedy, how fantastic soever, than to confess his necessary ignorance—a truth so disadvantageous to him. He cannot avoid owning that the senses are the sovereign lords of his knowledge; but they are uncertain, and falsifiable in all circumstances; 'tis there that he is to fight it out to the last; and if his just forces fail him, as they do, to supply that defect with obstinacy, temerity, and impudence. In case what the Epicureans say be true, viz: "that we have no knowledge if the senses' appearances be false;" and if that also be true which the Stoics say, "that the appearances of the senses are so false that they can furnish us with no manner of knowledge," we shall conclude, to the disadvantage of these two great dogmatical sects, that there is no science at all.

As to the error and uncertainty of the operation of the senses, every one may furnish himself with as many examples as he pleases; so ordinary are the faults and tricks they put upon us. In the echo of a valley the sound of a trumpet seems to meet us, which comes from a place behind:—

Exstantesque procul medio de gurgite montes,

Classibus inter qnos liber patet exitus, idem

Apparent, et longe divolsi licet, ingens

Insula conjunctis tamen ex his ana videtur...

Et fugere ad puppim colies campique videntur,

Qnos agimns proter navim, velisque volamus....

Ubi in medio nobis equus acer obhsit

Flamine, equi corpus transversum ferre videtur

Vis, et in adversum flumen contrudere raptim.

   "And rocks i' th' seas that proudly raise their head,

Though far disjoined, though royal navies spread,

Their sails between; yet if from distance shown,

They seem an island all combin'd in one.

Thus ships, though driven by a prosperous gale,

Seem fix'd to sailors; those seem under sail

That ride at anchor safe; and all admire,

As they row by, to see the rocks retire.

Thus, when in rapid streams my horse hath stood,

And I look'd downward on the rolling flood;

Though he stood still, I thought he did divide

The headlong streams, and strive against the tide,

And all things seem'd to move on every side."

Take a musket-ball under the forefinger, the middle finger being lapped over it, it feels so like two that a man will have much ado to persuade himself there is but one; the end of the two fingers feeling each of them one at the same time; for that the senses are very often masters of our reason, and constrain it to receive impressions which it judges and knows to be false, is frequently seen. I set aside the sense of feeling, that has its functions nearer, more lively, and substantial, that so often, by the effects of the pains it helps the body to, subverts and overthrows all those fine Stoical resolutions, and compels him to cry out of his belly, who has resolutely established this doctrine in his soul—"That the colic, and all other pains and diseases, are indifferent things, not having the power to abate any thing of the sovereign felicity wherein the wise man is seated by his virtue." There is no heart so effeminate that the rattle and sound of our drums and trumpets will not inflame with courage; nor so sullen that the harmony of our music will not rouse and cheer; nor so stubborn a soul that will not feel itself struck with some reverence in considering the gloomy vastness of our churches, the variety of ornaments, and order of our ceremonies; and in hearing the solemn music of our organs, and the grace and devout harmony of our voices. Even those that come in with contempt feel a certain shivering in their hearts, and something of dread that makes them begin to doubt their opinions. For my part I do not think myself strong enough to hear an ode of Horace or Catullus sung by a beautiful young mouth without emotion; and Zeno had reason to say "that the voice was the flower of beauty." One would once make me believe that a certain person, whom all we Frenchmen know, had imposed upon me in repeating some verses that he had made; that they were not the same upon paper that they were in the air; and that my eyes would make a contrary judgment to my ears; so great a power has pronunciation to give fashion and value to works that are left to the efficacy and modulation of the voice. And therefore Philoxenus was not so much to blame, hearing one giving an ill accent to some composition of his, in spurning and breaking certain earthen vessels of his, saying, "I break what is thine, because thou corruptest what is mine." To what end did those men who have, with a firm resolution, destroyed themselves, turn away their faces that they might not see the blow that was by themselves appointed? And that those who, for their health, desire and command incisions to be made, and cauteries to be applied to them, cannot endure the sight of the preparations, instruments, and operations of the surgeon, being that the sight is not in any way to participate in the pain? Are not these proper examples to verify the authority the senses have over the imagination? 'Tis to much purpose that we know these tresses were borrowed from a page or a lackey; that this rouge came from Spain, and this pearl-powder from the Ocean Sea. Our sight will, nevertheless, compel us to confess their subject more agreeable and more lovely against all reason; for in this there is nothing of its own:—

Auferinrar cultu; gemmis, auroque teguntur

Crimina; pars minima est ipsa puella sni.

Spe, ubi sit quod ames, inter tarn multa requiras:

Decipit hac oculos gide dives Amor.

"By dress we're won; gold, gems, and rich brocades

Make up the pageant that your heart invades;

In all that glittering figure which you see,

The far least part of her own self is she;

In vain for her you love amidst such cost

You search, the mistress in such dress is lost."

What a strange power do the poets attribute to the senses, that make Narcissus so desperately in love with his own shadow,

> Cunctaque miratur, quibus est mirabilis ipse;
>
> Se cupit imprudens, et, qui probat, ipse probatur;
>
> Dumque petit, petitur; pariterque accendit, et ardet:

> "Admireth all; for which to be admired;
>
> And inconsiderately himself desir'd.
>
> The praises which he gives his beauty claim'd,
>
> Who seeks is sought, th' inflamer is inflam'd:"

and Pygmalion's judgment so troubled by the impression of the sight of his ivory statue that he loves and adores it as if it were a living woman!

> Oscnla dat, reddique putat: sequi turque, tenetque,
>
> Et credit tactis digitos insidere membris;
>
> Et metuit, pressos veniat ne livor in artus.

> "He kisses, and believes he's kissed again;
>
> Seizes, and 'twixt his arms his love doth strain,
>
> And thinks the polish'd ivory thus held
>
> Doth to his fingers amorous pressure yield,
>
> And has a timorous fear, lest black and blue
>
> Should in the parts with ardour press'd ensue."

Put a philosopher into a cage of small thin set bars of iron, hang him on the top of the high tower of Notre Dame at Paris; he will see, by manifest reason, that he cannot possibly fall, and yet he will find (unless he has been used to the plumber's trade) that he cannot help but the sight of the excessive height will fright and astound him; for we have enough to do to assure ourselves in the galleries of our steeples, if they are made with open work, although they are of stone; and some there are that cannot endure so much as to think of it. Let there be a beam thrown over betwixt these two towers, of breadth sufficient to walk upon, there is no philosophical wisdom so firm that can give us the courage to walk over it as we should do upon the ground. I have often tried this upon our mountains in these parts; and though I am one who am not the most subject to be afraid, I was not able to endure to look into that infinite depth without horror and trembling, though I stood above my length from the edge of the precipice, and could not have fallen unless I would. Where I also observed that, what height soever the precipice was, provided there were some tree, or some jutting out of a rock, a little to support and divide the sight, it a little eases our fears, and gives greater assurance; as if they were things by which in falling we might have some relief; but that direct precipices we are not to look upon without being giddy; Ut despici vine vertigine timid ocvlorum animique non possit: "'To that one cannot look without dizziness;" which is a manifest imposture of the sight. And therefore it was that that fine philosopher put out his own eyes, to free the soul from being diverted by them, and that he might philosophize at greater liberty; but, by the same rule, he should have dammed up his ears, that Theophrastus says are the most dangerous instruments about us for receiving violent impressions to alter and disturb us; and, finally, should have deprived himself of all his other senses, that is to say, of his life and being; for they have all the power to command our soul and reason: Fit etiam sope specie qudam, sope vocum gravitate et cantibus, ut pettantur animi vehementius; sope etiam cura et timor, "For it often falls out that the minds are more vehemently struck by some sight, by the quality and sound of the voice, or by singing; and ofttimes also by grief and fear." Physicians hold that there are certain complexions that are agitated by the same sounds and instruments even to fury. I have seen some who could not hear a bone gnawed under the table without impatience; and there is scarce any man who is not disturbed at the sharp and shrill noise that the file makes in grating upon the iron; as also to hear chewing near them, or to hear any one speak who has an impediment in the throat or nose, will move some people even to anger and hatred. Of what use was that piping prompter of Gracchus, who softened, raised, and moved his master's voice whilst he declaimed at Rome, if the movements and quality of the sound had not the power to move and alter the judgments of the auditory? In earnest, there is wonderful reason to keep such a clutter about the firmness of this fine piece, that suffers itself to be turned and twined by the motion and accidents of so light a wind.

The same cheat that the senses put upon our understanding they have in turn put upon them; the soul also some times has its revenge; they lie and contend which should most deceive one another. What we see and hear when we are transported with passion, we neither see nor hear as it is:—

Et solem geminum, et duplices se ostendere Thebas.

"Thebes seems two cities, and the sun two suns."

The object that we love appears to us more beautiful than it really is;

    Multimodis igitur pravas turpesque videmus

  Esse in deliciis, summoque in honore vigere;

  "Hence 'tis that ugly things in fancied dress

  Seem gay, look fair to lovers' eyes, and please;"

and that we hate more ugly; to a discontented and afflicted man the light of the day seems dark and overcast. Our senses are not only depraved, but very often stupefied by the passions of the soul; how many things do we see that we do not take notice of, if the mind be occupied with other thoughts?

    In rebus quoque apertis noscere possis,

  Si non advertas animum, proinde esse quasi omni

  Tempore semot fuerint, longeque remot:

  "Nay, even in plainest things, unless the mind

  Take heed, unless she sets herself to find,

  The thing no more is seen, no more belov'd,

  Than if the most obscure and most remov'd:"

it would appear that the soul retires within, and amuses the powers of the senses. And so both the inside and the outside of man is full of infirmity and falsehood.

They who have compared our lives to a dream were, perhaps, more in the right than they were aware of. When we dream, the soul lives, works, and exercises all its faculties, neither more nor less than when awake; but more largely and obscurely, yet not so much, neither, that the difference should be as great as betwixt night and the meridian brightness of the sun, but as betwixt night and shade; there she sleeps, here she slumbers; but, whether more or less, 'tis still dark, and Cimmerian darkness. We wake sleeping, and sleep waking. I do not see so clearly in my sleep; but as to my being awake, I never found it clear enough and free from clouds; moreover, sleep, when it is profound, sometimes rocks even dreams themselves asleep; but our waking is never so sprightly that it rightly purges and dissipates those whimsies, which are waking dreams, and worse than dreams. Our reason and soul receiving those fancies and opinions that come in dreams, and authorizing the actions of our dreams with the like approbation that they do those of the day, wherefore do we not doubt whether our thought, our action, is not another sort of dreaming, and our waking a certain kind of sleep?

If the senses be our first judges, it is not ours that we are alone to consult; for, in this faculty, beasts have as great, or greater, than we; it is certain that some of them have the sense of hearing more quick than man; others that of seeing, others that of feeling, others that of touch and taste. Democritus said, that the gods and brutes had the sensitive faculties more perfect than man. But betwixt the effects of their senses and ours the difference is extreme. Our spittle cleanses and dries up our wounds; it kills the serpent:—

> Tantaque in his rebas distantia differitasque est,
>
> Ut quod aliis cibus est, aliis fuat acre venenum.
>
> Spe etenim serpens, hominis contacta saliv,
>
> Disperit, ac sese mandendo conficit ipsa:

> "And in those things the difference is so great
>
> That what's one's poison is another's meat;
>
> For serpents often have been seen, 'tis said,
>
> When touch'd with human spittle, to go mad,
>
> And bite themselves to death:"

what quality shall we attribute to our spittle? as it affects ourselves, or as it affects the serpent? By which of the two senses shall we prove the true essence that we seek for?

Pliny says there are certain sea-hares in the Indies that are poison to us, and we to them; insomuch that, with the least touch, we kill them. Which shall be truly poison, the man or the fish? Which shall we believe, the fish of the man, or the man of the fish? One quality of the air infects a man, that does the ox no harm; some other infects the ox, but hurts not the man. Which of the two shall, in truth and nature, be the pestilent quality? To them who have the jaundice, all things seem yellow and paler than to us:—

> Lurida prterea fiunt, qucunque tuentur Arquati.

> "Besides, whatever jaundic'd eyes do view

Looks pale as well as those, and yellow too."

They who are troubled with the disease that the physicians call hyposphagma—which is a suffusion of blood under the skin—see all things red and bloody. What do we know but that these humours, which thus alter the operations of sight, predominate in beasts, and are usual with them? for we see some whose eyes are yellow, like us who have the jaundice; and others of a bloody colour; 'tis likely that the colours of objects seem other to them than to us. Which of the two shall make a right judgment? for it is not said that the essence of things has a relation to man only; hardness, whiteness, depth, and sharpness, have reference to the service and knowledge of animals as well as to us, and nature has equally designed them for their use. When we press down the eye, the body that we look upon we perceive to be longer and more extended;—many beasts have their eyes so pressed down; this length, therefore, is perhaps the true form of that body, and not that which our eyes give it in the usual state. If we close the lower part of the eye things appear double to us:—

Bina lucemarum fiorentia lumina flammis...

Et duplices hominum facis, et corpora bina.

"One lamp seems double, and the men appear

Each on two bodies double heads to bear."

If our ears be hindered, or the passage stopped with any thing, we receive the sound quite otherwise than we usually do; animals, likewise, who have either the ears hairy, or but a very little hole instead of an ear, do not, consequently, hear as we do, but receive another kind of sound. We see at festivals and theatres that, opposing a painted glass of a certain colour to the light of the flambeaux, all things in the place appear to us green, yellow, or violet:—

Et vulgo faciunt id lutea russaque vela,

Et ferrugina, cum, magnis intenta theatris,

Per malos vulgata trabesque, trementia pendent;

Namque ibi consessum caveai subter, et omnem

Scenai speciem, patrum, matrumque, deorumque

Inficiunt, coguntque suo volitare colore:

"Thus when pale curtains, or the deeper red,

O'er all the spacious theatre are spread,

Which mighty masts and sturdy pillars bear,

And the loose curtains wanton in the air;

Whole streams of colours from the summit flow,

The rays divide them in their passage through,

And stain the scenes, and men, and gods below:"

'tis likely that the eyes of animals, which we see to be of divers colours, produce the appearance of bodies the same with their eyes.

We should, therefore, to make a right judgment of the oppositions of the senses, be first agreed with beasts, and secondly amongst ourselves; which we by no means are, but enter into dispute every time that one hears, sees, or tastes something otherwise than another does, and contests, as much as upon any other thing, about the diversity of the images that the senses represent to us. A child, by the ordinary rule of nature, hears, sees, and talks otherwise than a man of thirty years old; and he than one of threescore. The senses are, in some, more obscure and dusky, and more open and quick in others. We receive things variously, according as we are, and according as they appear to us. Those rings which are cut out in the form of feathers, which are called endless feathers, no eye can discern their size, or can keep itself from the deception that on one side they enlarge, and on the other contract, and come So a point, even when the ring is being turned round the finger; yet, when you feel them, they seem all of an equal size. Now, our perception being so uncertain and so controverted, it is no more a wonder if we are told that we may declare that snow appears white to us; but that to affirm that it is in its own essence really so is more than we are able to justify; and, this foundation being shaken, all the knowledge in the world must of necessity fall to ruin. What! do our senses themselves hinder one another? A picture seems raised and embossed to the sight; in the handling it seems flat to the touch. Shall we say that musk, which delights the smell, and is offensive to the taste, is agreeable or no? There are herbs and unguents proper for one part o the body, that are hurtful to another; honey is pleasant to the taste, but offensive to the sight. They who, to assist their lust, used in ancient times to make use of magnifying-glasses to represent the members they were to employ bigger, by that ocular tumidity to please themselves the more; to which of their senses did they give the prize,—whether to the sight, that represented the members as large and great as they would desire, or to the feeling, which represented them little and contemptible? Are they our senses that supply the subject with these different conditions, and have the subjects themselves, nevertheless, but one? As we see in the bread we eat, it is nothing but bread, but, by being eaten, it becomes bones, blood, flesh, hair; and nails:—

    Ut cibus in membra atque artus cum diditur omnes,

Disperit,, atque aliam naturam sufficit ex se;

    "As meats, diffus'd through all the members, lose

Their former state, and different things compose;"

the humidity sucked up by the root of a tree becomes trunk, leaf, and fruit; and the air, being but one, is modulated, in a trumpet, to a thousand sorts of sounds; are they our senses, I would fain know, that, in like manner, form these subjects into so many divers qualities, or have they them really such in themselves? And upon this doubt what can we determine of their true essence? Moreover, since the accidents of disease, of raving, or sleep, make things appear otherwise to us than they do to the healthful, the wise, and those that are awake, is it not likely that our right posture of health and understanding, and our natural humours, have, also, wherewith to give a being to things that have a relation to their own condition, and accommodate them to themselves, as well as when they are disordered;—that health is as capable of giving them an aspect as sickness? Why has not the temperate a certain form of objects relative to it, as well as the intemperate? and why may it not as well stamp it with its own character as the other? He whose mouth is out of taste, says the wine is flat; the healthful man commends its flavour, and the thirsty its briskness. Now, our condition always accommodating things to itself, and transforming them according to its own posture, we cannot know what things truly are in themselves, seeing that nothing comes to us but what is falsified and altered by the senses. Where the compass, the square, and the rule, are crooked, all propositions drawn thence, and all buildings erected by those guides, must, of necessity, be also defective; the uncertainty of our senses renders every thing uncertain that they produce:—

    Denique ut in fabric, si prava est rgula prima,

Normaque si fallax rectis regionibus exit,

Et libella aliqu si ex parte claudicat hilum;

Omnia mendose fieri, atque obstipa necessum est,

Prava, cubantia, prona, supina, atque absona tecta;

Jam ruere ut qudam videantux'velle, ruantque

Prodita judiciis fallacibus omnia primis;

Sic igitur ratio tibi reram prava necesse est,

Falsaque sit, falsis qucunque ab sensibus orta est.

"But lastly, as in building, if the line

Be not exact and straight, the rule decline,

Or level false, how vain is the design!

Uneven, an ill-shap'd and tottering wall

Must rise; this part must sink, that part must fall,

Because the rules were false that fashion'd all;

Thus reason's rules are false if all commence

And rise from failing and from erring sense."

As to what remains, who can be fit to judge of and to determine those differences? As we say in controversies of religion that we must have a judge neither inclining to the one side nor the other, free from all choice and affection, which cannot be amongst Christians, just so it falls out in this; for if he be old he cannot judge of the sense of old age, being himself a party in the case; if young, there is the same exception; if healthful, sick, asleep, or awake, he is still the same incompetent judge. We must have some one exempt from all these propositions, as of things indifferent to him; and by this rule we must have a judge that never was.

To judge of the appearances that we receive of subjects, we ought t have a deciding instrument; to verify this instrument we must have demonstration; to verify this demonstration an instrument; and here we are round again upon the wheel, and no further advanced. Seeing the senses cannot determine our dispute, being full of uncertainty themselves, it must then be reason that must do it; but no reason can be erected upon any other foundation than that of another reason; and so we run back to all infinity. Our fancy does not apply itself to things that are strange, but is conceived by the mediation of the senses; and the senses do not comprehend a foreign subject, but only their own passions; by which means fancy and appearance are no part of the subject, but only of the passion and sufferance of sense; which passion and subject are different things; wherefore whoever judges by appearances judges by another thing than the subject. And to say that the passions of the senses convey to the soul the quality of foreign subjects by resemblance, how can the soul and understanding be assured of this resemblance, having of itself no commerce with foreign subjects? As they who never knew Socrates cannot, when they see his picture, say it is like him. Now, whoever would, notwithstanding, judge by appearances, if it be by all, it is impossible, because they hinder one another by their contrarieties and discrepancies, as we by experience see: shall some select appearances govern the rest? you must verify this select by another select, the second by a third, and thus there will never be any end to it. Finally, there is no constant existence, neither of the objects' being nor our own; both we, and our judgments, and all mortal things, are evermore incessantly running and rolling; and consequently nothing certain can be established from the one to the other, both the judging and the judged being in a continual motion and mutation.

We have no communication with being, by reason that all human nature is always in the middle, betwixt being bom and dying, giving but an obscure appearance and shadow, a weak and uncertain opinion of itself; and if, perhaps, you fix your thought to apprehend your being, it would be but like grasping water; for the more you clutch your hand to squeeze and hold what is in its own nature flowing, so much more you lose of what you would grasp and hold. So, seeing that all things are subject to pass from one change to another, reason, that there looks for a real substance, finds itself deceived, not being able to apprehend any thing that is subsistent and permanent, because that every thing is either entering into being, and is not yet arrived at it, or begins to die before it is bom. Plato said, that bodies had never any existence, but only birth; conceiving that Homer had made the Ocean and Thetis father and mother of the gods, to show us that all things are in a perpetual fluctuation, motion, and variation; the opinion of all the philosophers, as he says, before his time, Parmenides only excepted, who would not allow things to have motion, on the power whereof he sets a mighty value. Pythagoras was of opinion that all matter was flowing and unstable; the Stoics, that there is no time present, and that what we call so is nothing but the juncture and meeting of the future and the past; Heraclitus, that never any man entered twice into the same river; Epichar-mus, that he who borrowed money but an hour ago does not owe it now; and that he who was invited over-night to come the next day to dinner comes nevertheless uninvited, considering that they are no more the same men, but are become others; and that there could not a mortal substance be found twice in the same condition; for, by the suddenness and quickness of the change, it one while disperses, and another reunites; it comes and goes after such a manner that what begins to be born never arrives to the perfection of being, forasmuch as that birth is never finished and never stays, as being at an end, but from the seed is evermore changing and shifting one to another; as human seed is first in the mother's womb made a formless embryo, after delivered thence a sucking infant, afterwards it becomes a boy, then a youth, then a man, and at last a decrepit old man; so that age and subsequent generation is always destroying and spoiling that which went before:—

Mutt enira mundi naturam totius tas,

Ex alioque alius status excipere omnia debet;

Nec manet ulla sui similis res; omnia migrant,

Omnia commutt natura, et vertere cogit.

"For time the nature of the world translates,

And from preceding gives all things new states;

Nought like itself remains, but all do range,

And nature forces every thing to change."

"And yet we foolishly fear one kind of death, whereas we have already passed, and do daily pass, so many others; for not only, as Heraclitus said, the death of fire is generation of air, and the death of air generation of water; but, moreover, we may more manifestly discern it in ourselves; manhood dies, and passes away when age comes on; and youth is terminated in the flower of age of a full-grown man, infancy in youth, and the first age dies in infancy; yesterday died in to-day, and to-day will die in to-morrow; and there is nothing that remains in the same state, or that is always the same thing. And that it is so let this be the proof; if we are always one and the same, how comes it to pass that we are now pleased with one thing, and by and by with another? How comes it to pass that we love or hate contrary things, that we praise or condemn them? How comes it to pass that we have different affections, and no more retain the same sentiment in the same thought? For it is not likely that without mutation we should assume other passions; and, that which suffers mutation does not remain the same, and if it be not the same it is not at all; but the same that the being is does, like it, unknowingly change and alter; becoming evermore another from another thing; and consequently the natural senses abuse and deceive themselves, taking that which seems for that which is, for want of well knowing what that which is, is. But what is it then that truly is? That which is eternal; that is to say, that never had beginning, nor never shall have ending, and to which time can bring no mutation. For time is a mobile thine, and that appears as in a shadow, with a matter evermore flowing and running, without ever remaining stable and permanent; and to which belong those words, before and after, has been, or shall be: which at the first sight, evidently show that it is not a thing that is; for it were a great folly, and a manifest falsity, to say that that is which is not et being, or that has already ceased to be. And as to these words, present, instant, and now, by which it seems that we principally support and found the intelligence of time, reason, discovering, does presently destroy it; for it immediately divides and splits it into the future and past, being of necessity to consider it divided in two. The same happens to nature, that is measured, as to time that measures it; for she has nothing more subsisting and permanent than the other, but all things are either born, bearing, or dying. So that it were sinful to say of God, who is he only who is, that he was, or that he shall be ; for those are terms of declension, transmutation, and vicissitude, of what cannot continue or remain in being; wherefore we are to conclude that God alone is, not according to any measure of time, but according to an immutable and an immovable eternity, not measured by time, nor subject to any declension; before whom nothing was, and after whom nothing shall be, either more new or more recent, but a real being, that with one sole now fills the for ever, and that there is nothing that truly is but he alone; without our being able to say, he has been, or shall be; without beginning, and without end." To this so religious conclusion of a pagan I shall only add this testimony of one of the same condition, for the close of this long and tedious discourse, which would furnish me with endless matter: "What a vile and abject thing," says he, "is man, if he do not raise himself above humanity!" 'Tis a good word and a profitable desire, but withal absurd; for to make the handle bigger than the hand, the cubic longer than the arm, and to hope to stride further than our legs can reach, is both impossible and monstrous; or that man should rise above himself and humanity; for he cannot see but with his eyes, nor seize but with his hold. He shall be exalted, if God will lend him an extraordinary hand; he shall exalt himself, by abandoning and renouncing his own proper means, and by suffering himself to be raised and elevated by means purely celestial. It belongs to our Christian faith, and not to the stoical virtue, to pretend to that divine and miraculous metamorphosis.

MLA Style Citations for Scholarly Secondary Sources, Peer-Reviewed Journal Articles and Critical Essays

Abecassis, Jack I. "'Le Maire Et Montaigne Ont Tousjours Esté Deux, d'Une Separation Bien Claire': Public Necessity and Private Freedom in Montaigne." *MLN*, vol. 110, no. 5, 1995, pp. 1067–1089., www.jstor.org/stable/3251391.

Berry, Jessica N. "The Pyrrhonian Revival in Montaigne and Nietzsche." *Journal of the History of Ideas*, vol. 65, no. 3, 2004, pp. 497–514., www.jstor.org/stable/3654143.

Bonadeo, Alfredo. "Montaigne on War." *Journal of the History of Ideas*, vol. 46, no. 3, 1985, pp. 417–426., www.jstor.org/stable/2709476.

Brown, Frieda S. "Montaigne and Gide's La Porte Étroite." *PMLA*, vol. 82, no. 1, 1967, pp. 136–141., www.jstor.org/stable/461058.

Chambers, Frank M. "Pascal's Montaigne." *PMLA*, vol. 65, no. 5, 1950, pp. 790–804., www.jstor.org/stable/459574.

Charron, Jean Daniel. "Did Charron Plagiarize Montaigne?" *The French Review*, vol. 34, no. 4, 1961, pp. 344–351., www.jstor.org/stable/383839.

Cons, Louis. "Présence De Montaigne." *The French Review*, vol. 6, no. 5, 1933, pp. 357–367., www.jstor.org/stable/380185.

Defaux, Gérard. "Une Leçon De Scepticisme: Montaigne, Le Monde Et Les Grands Hommes." *MLN*, vol. 116, no. 4, 2001, pp. 644–665., www.jstor.org/stable/3251752.

De Lutri, Joseph R. "Montaigne on the Noble Savage: A Shift in Perspective." *The French Review*, vol. 49, no. 2, 1975, pp. 206–211., www.jstor.org/stable/388691.

Demure, Catherine, and Dianne Sears. "Montaigne: The Paradox and the Miracle-Structure and Meaning in 'The Apology for Raymond Sebond' (Essais II:12)." *Yale French Studies*, no. 64, 1983, pp. 188–208., www.jstor.org/stable/2929958.

Force, Pierre. "Montaigne and the Coherence of Eclecticism." *Journal of the History of Ideas*, vol. 70, no. 4, 2009, pp. 523–544., www.jstor.org/stable/20621910.

Frame, Donald M. "What Next in Montaigne Studies?" *The French Review*, vol. 36, no. 6, 1963, pp. 577–587., www.jstor.org/stable/383673.

Gillespie, Michael Allen. "Montaigne's Humanistic Liberalism." *The Journal of Politics*, vol. 47, no. 1, 1985, pp. 140–159., www.jstor.org/stable/2131069.

Glidden, Hope H. "The Face in the Text: Montaigne's Emblematic Self-Portrait (Essais III:12)." *Renaissance Quarterly*, vol. 46, no. 1, 1993, pp. 71–97., www.jstor.org/stable/3039148.

Gray, Floyd. "Reflexions on Charron's Debt to Montaigne." *The French Review*, vol. 35, no. 4, 1962, pp. 377–382., www.jstor.org/stable/383358.

Griffin, Robert. "Title, Structure and Theme of Montaigne's 'Des Coches.'" *MLN*, vol. 82, no. 3, 1967, pp. 285–290., www.jstor.org/stable/2908440.

Grundy, Dominick. "Skepticism in Two Essays by Montaigne and Sir Thomas Browne." *Journal of the History of Ideas*, vol. 34, no. 4, 1973, pp. 529–542., www.jstor.org/stable/2708886.

Guaragnella, Pasquale. "Paolo Sarpi Fra Montaigne e Charron." *MLN*, vol. 120, no. 1, 2005, pp. 173–189., www.jstor.org/stable/3252033.

Hamlin, William M. "Florio's Montaigne and the Tyranny of 'Custome': Appropriation, Ideology, and Early English Readership of the *Essayes*." *Renaissance Quarterly*, vol. 63, no. 2, 2010, pp. 491–544., www.jstor.org/stable/10.1086/655233.

Hampton, Timothy. "Montaigne and the Body of Socrates: Narrative and Exemplarity in the Essais." *MLN*, vol. 104, no. 4, 1989, pp. 880–898., www.jstor.org/stable/2905269.

HANDLER-SPITZ, Rivi. "Provocative Texts: Li Zhi, Montaigne, and the Promotion of Critical Judgment in Early Modern Readers." *Chinese Literature: Essays, Articles, Reviews (CLEAR)*, vol. 35, 2013, pp. 123–153., www.jstor.org/stable/43490165.

Henderson, W. B. Drayton. "MONTAIGNE'S 'APOLOGIE OF RAYMOND SEBOND', AND 'KING LEAR.'" *The Shakespeare Association Bulletin*, vol. 14, no. 4, 1939, pp. 209–225., www.jstor.org/stable/23675637.

Henry, Patrick. "Pygmalion in the Essais: 'De l'Affection Des Pères Aux Enfans.'" *The French Review*, vol. 68, no. 2, 1994, pp. 229–238., www.jstor.org/stable/396355.

Hoffmann, George. "The Montaigne Monopoly: Revising the Essais under the French Privilege System." *PMLA*, vol. 108, no. 2, 1993, pp. 308–319., www.jstor.org/stable/462600.

Hoffmann, George. "Anatomy of the Mass: Montaigne's 'Cannibals.'" *PMLA*, vol. 117, no. 2, 2002, pp. 207–221., www.jstor.org/stable/823269.

Hovey, Kenneth Alan. "'Mountaigny Saith Prettily': Bacon's French and the Essay." *PMLA*, vol. 106, no. 1, 1991, pp. 71–82., www.jstor.org/stable/462824.

Jordan, Constance. "Montaigne on Property, Public Service, and Political Servitude." *Renaissance Quarterly*, vol. 56, no. 2, 2003, pp. 408–435., www.jstor.org/stable/1261852.

Keller, Abraham C. "Montaigne on the Dignity of Man." *PMLA*, vol. 72, no. 1, 1957, pp. 43–54., www.jstor.org/stable/460217.

Kellermann, Frederick. "Montaigne, Reader of Plato." *Comparative Literature*, vol. 8, no. 4, 1956, pp. 307–322., www.jstor.org/stable/1768763.

Kirsch, Arthur. "Virtue, Vice, and Compassion in Montaigne and The Tempest." *Studies in English Literature, 1500-1900*, vol. 37, no. 2, 1997, pp. 337–352., www.jstor.org/stable/450837.

Knee, Philip. "La Critique De La Politique Dans Les Essais: Montaigne Et Machiavel." *Canadian Journal of Political Science / Revue Canadienne De Science Politique*, vol. 33, no. 4, 2000, pp. 691–722., www.jstor.org/stable/3232660.

Kurz, Harry. "Montaigne and La Boétie in the Chapter on Friendship." *PMLA*, vol. 65, no. 4, 1950, pp. 483–530., www.jstor.org/stable/459652.

MacPhail, Eric. "In the Wake of Solon: Memory and Modernity in the Essays of Montaigne." *MLN*, vol. 113, no. 4, 1998, pp. 881–896., www.jstor.org/stable/3251407.

Miernowski, Jan. "The Law of Non-Contradiction and French Renaissance Literature: Skepticism and Negative Theology." *South Central Review*, vol. 10, no. 2, 1993, pp. 49–66., www.jstor.org/stable/3189999.

Moser, Patrick. "Literary Identity in Montaigne's 'Apologie De Raimond Sebond.'" *The French Review*, vol. 77, no. 4, 2004, pp. 716–727., www.jstor.org/stable/25479460.

Nemser, Ruby. "Nosce Teipsum and the Essais of Montaigne." *Studies in English Literature, 1500-1900*, vol. 16, no. 1, 1976, pp. 95–103., www.jstor.org/stable/449857.

Norton, Grace. "The Use Made by Montaigne of Some Special Words." *Modern Language Notes*, vol. 20, no. 8, 1905, pp. 243–248., www.jstor.org/stable/2917525.

O'Rourke Boyle, Marjorie. "Montaigne's Consubstantial Book." *Renaissance Quarterly*, vol. 50, no. 3, 1997, pp. 723–749., www.jstor.org/stable/3039260.

Rendall, Steven. "Montaigne under the Sign of Fama." *Yale French Studies*, no. 66, 1984, pp. 137–159., www.jstor.org/stable/2929868.

Rigolot, François. "Curiosity, Contingency, and Cultural Diversity: Montaigne's Readings at the Vatican Library." *Renaissance Quarterly*, vol. 64, no. 3, 2011, pp. 847–874., www.jstor.org/stable/10.1086/662851.

Rigolot, François. "1492, 1592, 1992: Questions d'Anniversaires-Montaigne Et l'Amérique." *The French Review*, vol. 67, no. 1, 1993, pp. 1–11., www.jstor.org/stable/397779.

Schaefer, David Lewis. "The Good, the Beautiful, and the Useful: Montaigne's Transvaluation of Values." *The American Political Science Review*, vol. 73, no. 1, 1979, pp. 139–154., www.jstor.org/stable/1954737.

Schiffman, Zachary S. "Montaigne and the Rise of Skepticism in Early Modern Europe: A Reappraisal." *Journal of the History of Ideas*, vol. 45, no. 4, 1984, pp. 499–516., www.jstor.org/stable/2709370.

Sedley, David L. "Sublimity and Skepticism in Montaigne." *PMLA*, vol. 113, no. 5, 1998, pp. 1079–1092., www.jstor.org/stable/463243.

Szabari, Antonia. "'Parler Seulement De Moy': The Disposition of the Subject in Montaigne's Essay 'De l'Art De Conferer.'" *MLN*, vol. 116, no. 5, 2001, pp. 1001–1024., www.jstor.org/stable/3251793.

Temple, Maud Elizabeth. "Montaigne Differentia." *Studies in Philology*, vol. 19, no. 4, 1922, pp. 357–361., www.jstor.org/stable/4171833.

Tournon, André, and Matthew Senior. "Self-Interpretation in Montaigne's Essais." *Yale French Studies*, no. 64, 1983, pp. 51–72., www.jstor.org/stable/2929950.

West, William N. "Reading Rooms: Architecture and Agency in the Houses of Michel De Montaigne and Nicholas Bacon." *Comparative Literature*, vol. 56, no. 2, 2004, pp. 111–129., www.jstor.org/stable/4125444.

Wiesmann, Marc-André. "Intertextual Labyrinths: Ariadne's Lament in Montaigne's 'Sur Des Vers De Virgile.'" *Renaissance Quarterly*, vol. 53, no. 3, 2000, pp. 792–820., www.jstor.org/stable/290149

Made in the USA
Coppell, TX
09 October 2021